MW01222580

HEY MUM, IT'S ME

A Story of Connection
and the Lessons Learned

BY SUSAN ROSS MScN

suross@tru.ca

 FriesenPress

Suite 300 - 990 Fort St
Victoria, BC, V8V 3K2
Canada

www.friesenpress.com

Copyright © 2021 by Susan Ross
First Edition — 2021

ISBN
978-1-5255-9224-9 (Hardcover)
978-1-5255-9223-2 (Paperback)
978-1-5255-9225-6 (eBook)

Self-Help, Death, Grief, Bereavement

Distributed to the trade by The Ingram Book Company

Table of Contents

Dedicated to
James Gregory Ross
1973–2002

Sent from God's hands
Straight from heaven
A beautiful ray of light

 Spirit Everlasting

Introduction

Death. It's such an ugly word. We turn our heads away from it because it's something we all tend to fear. We want to concentrate on life and living, not death and dying. How can we have one without the other? It's a dichotomy that follows us all our living years. We know death waits in the shadows, but that's where we want it—hidden. Out of sight, out of mind. It's a comfortable arrangement. It's *life* we want to think about.

We grow up with this mindset. When we're under the age of five, death is not seen as irreversible. It's not final. Just take a look at cartoons on a Saturday morning and you'll see characters running off cliffs or being run over by steamrollers only to bounce up again and carry on with the next great adventure. I smile when I think of the Road Runner and all the times he perished only to reappear in the next clip. No wonder children think this is how it works. Usually it's not until the age of nine that children begin to understand death is universal, inevitable and final. There's a realization it can happen to them and those they love.

Parents may feel they want to protect their children from death, so they don't include them in conversations about the impending death of someone they know. They may exclude them from funeral preparations, not let them go to the funeral. It wasn't always like this. If they lived in the 1800s, Grandma would have died at home, been washed and dressed by the women of the family, and laid on the dining room table for others to come and view her body. Death was closer in those days. The men of the community would build the coffin and carry Grandma to the cemetery. They would also prepare the burial site. Children and grandchildren would be included every step of the way. Death would not have been such a stranger.

Now death is quarantined in hospitals and hospices. Some people do die in their homes, but most tend to die in institutions. Strangers—funeral home attendants—come and take the body to be prepared for burial or cremation. If there's a funeral, these capable strangers make the arrangements and often conduct the service. This isn't true in every case, but it's a norm in today's society. Most of us have been marinated in this way of thinking.

When a person of significance leaves your life, it's a harsh blow. It's an assault on your belief that everything is okay. It becomes "not okay" very quickly as the impact invades your fragile sense of security. All our lives, we hear about people dying. We're inundated right from childhood with television images of war, gangland murders and global disasters. We see people tortured in foreign countries and others murdered. It comes right into our living rooms.

Online games are prolific with the same dark images and we actually pay to see them. Even children's books carry the theme of death. I have many editions of *Little Red Riding Hood*—purchased because I was fascinated with the variety of endings. In early versions, the wolf sneaks into Grandma's house, kills her and then butchers her. He pours her blood into a bottle and slices her flesh like luncheon meat and puts it on a platter. When Red Riding Hood arrives, he offers it to her as a refreshment.

In the 19th century, Brothers Grimm wrote about Red Riding Hood and Grandma being eaten by the wolf. The woodsman appears and cuts the wolf open, and out they pop. The woodsman then fills the wolf's stomach with big rocks while the wolf sleeps. When he wakes up, he collapses and dies.

Can you imagine what goes through the minds of little children as these scenarios are woven into their reality? Indeed, death is a part of growing up. We seem to just accept the stories we hear, whether on the news or in the stories we read. Death is viewed from a distance, from the comfort of our home. We go on living our days and subliminally absorb these grim events into our subconscious landscape and shut the door. We don't want to think about death.

If life is all we consider in our day-to-day thinking, it's not surprising death hits us hard when it happens. As a registered nurse, I've had the privilege of being present for many, many deaths. Some have been difficult, especially when the person struggles near the end. Others have been so peaceful. There have been people, as they near the end, who reach out or call out to those unseen. The first time I witnessed it, the patient's wife told me her husband called out the name of their dead daughter. She found great comfort in knowing her husband could see and reach for their daughter. It was such an honour to be included in a beautiful and tender moment. I was fascinated by the possibility that a connection between people need not cease when death takes a life.

Something else happened regularly when I was in the room when a person died. At the moment of death, I could feel the energy move out of their body. The form in the bed still looked like the patient, but the life force was somewhere else. You could close your eyes and "feel" the life was gone. I've spoken to other nurses who told me they've experienced the same thing.

The more deaths I witnessed, the more I began to question what I'd been taught—or perhaps more accurately *not* taught—about death. Even as a child, death had intrigued me. It held a mystery that has followed me all my life.

I have written this book as a tool to shine some light on the shadow we call death. The world of Spirit offered me opportunities to let go of my early understanding about the finality of our existence. It opened up a world of possibilities. The experiences offered in these pages changed me; they brought me a very different perspective on life and death. It is my hope it will do the same for you.

This book is broken into three distinct parts. It's a path that begins in Part one, with a brief glimpse into my childhood and the elements that contributed to who I was. It moves to Part two to show the catastrophe that would forever change me and how I viewed life and death. In Part three, the path ends with who I am now and how I got there.

Part One:
This is Who I Was

CHAPTER 1

Childhood and Growing Up

When we are born, we start our lives with a clean slate. There's no history, no gender, no past that we know of. There's only an unlimited future. We come in squeaky clean, ready to embark on our life. As babies, we soon learn if our needs are met, we're happy. In the best scenario, we have parents who love and care for us, with sensitivity and continuity. When we're hungry, we are fed. When we're soiled, we are changed. If we become anxious, someone holds us, rocks us and tells us everything is okay. We learn to develop trust and begin to feel safe in the world.

I had a somewhat different experience.

I was born July 4 at 9:00 p.m., precisely. I was placed in a bassinet in the hall of my parents' home; there weren't enough bedrooms in the house for all of us. As my sister, Jocelyn, got there five years ahead of me, she got the second of two bedrooms. It didn't seem to bother me to sleep in the hall. My mother said she would watch my bassinet shake from side to side and when she looked in, I was full of joy, just happy to be alive.

My mother wasn't so happy and experienced many years of depression. She was a beautiful, charismatic person, but her disappointment in life created the perfect platform for her depressive disorder. On one hand, she saw herself as someone who deserved to be praised and loved. On the other hand, she lacked the understanding of how to first love and praise herself. So she was constantly disappointed in others for not reinforcing these elements in her life.

When I came along, I soon realized my high energy irritated her. As time went on, I began to understand just being happy and content wasn't enough. Admittedly, Mum did not particularly enjoy the role of motherhood, and her children grew up knowing this. I learned at an early age to contain my happiness. As the years went by, I began to see the world through my mother's eyes and realized it was not a safe place. It was most certainly not a place I could trust.

Along with depression, my mother developed anxiety, which was treated with a variety of medications including phenobarbital. The chemical reactions caused by this drug did nothing but exacerbate her already existing depression. When she was taking phenobarbital, she used it as a weapon. She would say to us, "If it wasn't for you, I wouldn't have to take this." This was confusing to me—I was trying my best and still it wasn't good enough.

I learned to be quiet and stay out of the way. I made myself small. I began to develop the persona of a child who was acutely aware of other people's feelings, especially my mother's. I was a child trying to survive in a world portrayed as dangerous and unpredictable. And I did it well! I became sensitive and intuitive, able to sense energies I couldn't see or hear. Sometimes it was just a feeling, as if I'd picked up a radio frequency from somewhere. It was a magical world. When I retreated inside myself, it was peaceful and calm. I was aware of a universe just outside my conscious mind, but at the time I didn't fully realize what it was.

Later in my life, I would understand my spiritual nature more fully. All I knew was it provided a place where I could rest. This was a good thing because during my childhood I was always on guard. Life was unpredictable. I was never quite sure where things were going. Sometimes everything seemed normal. Other times, when my parents were working through some problems, the children were either brought into it or ignored.

I looked for ways to keep the peace. I learned how to fold my own needs away to concentrate on the needs of others. In doing so, I unknowingly diminished myself. It wasn't a conscious action, but it protected and preserved the limited sense of security I felt as a child. Fear of abandonment was causing my behaviour. My strategies rested on striving to be accepted and loved in my family.

There's some interesting research on the subject of the connection between a child and their caretakers. John Bowlby's work in this field prompted Paul Strand[1] to investigate attachment theory, which looks at three forms of attachment between a child and a parent.

A secure attachment involves parenting that is continuous and predicable. In other words, when a child's in distress and needs attention, the parent provides the security, support and care with warmth and sensitivity. This child grows up to become an adult who is confident support will be available when needed. These children also demonstrate an optimism in life.

An insecure anxious attachment is created when parents intermittently provide care, perhaps without sensitivity and warmth. This behaviour intensifies a child's need to please in an effort to find a guarded sense of security. It's a bid to stop feeling afraid and anxious in hopes of feeling secure.

The final attachment style is insecure–avoidant. In this case, the child knows their parents will be unresponsive. They stop seeking security and develop a self-sufficiency that's compulsive. There's almost a numbing of feelings and a defensive leaning towards emotional independence.

I bring this up because I now understand that my family situation caused me, as a child, to develop an insecure–anxious attachment. It fostered the caretaking tendencies I had, which continued well into my adult life. A hypersensitivity developed as I searched for ways to gain acceptance.

I found I could put a temporary smile on my mother's face by taking on some of her daily tasks, like cooking and doing the laundry. I learned how to iron my father's shirts at a young age. I would first wash them. While they were still damp from the washer, I would roll them up and put them in the fridge in a plastic bag. That way, with the help of Easy-On Spray Starch, they would turn out perfectly crisp and ready to put in the closet. It gave me a sense of order and responsibility. I also learned how to cook almost anything. By the age of eleven, I was able to put a Thanksgiving dinner on the table with ease. This made my mother very happy. I'm thankful for this because, to this day, cooking is one of the best things in

---

[1] Paul S. Strand, "The security-seeking impulse and the unification of attachment and culture," *Psychological Review* (April 13, 2020), https://pubmed.ncbi.nlm.nih.gov/32281814/.

my life. I love to create beautiful meals for others and myself. Food has become one of my passions and I choose to thank my mother for this.

In stark contrast to my mother, my dad was a small, quiet man, who lived in the shadow of his colourful partner. He was a brilliant man. He came from a working-class family; his father was a shipbuilder. My mother came from a privileged family; her father was a medical doctor and her mother, a nurse. My grandfather and grandmother always believed my mother had married beneath herself and did not hesitate to share this opinion with anyone who would listen. My father worked hard but always fell short of what was expected. He was a true genius in every sense of the word. If there was a problem to solve, he would work until he found an answer. To me, his mind was amazing. He was a tender, sensitive and loving father. I was so blessed to have him in my life. But his gentle nature was often misunderstood by others. In my eyes, the world seemed to understand strong masculine men, often applauding them for their unemotional scrutiny of complex life events. But the men like my father could be overlooked because they didn't possess a loud aggressive manner and could get lost in the shuffle. I can remember, even as a small child, feeling responsible for buffering my dad from the harsh world and also from my mother's dominating energy.

When I was four, my brother, Peter, was born. This was the turning point for my father. He was overjoyed he had a son. He constructed a flagpole by our house and mounted a sky blue flag to announce the arrival. He was elated! From that day until the day he died in 1995, there was an unspoken reverence between these two souls. I was privileged to witness this special bond right in my own family. I was so glad my dad found some happiness in his life.

My mum found a third child more of a burden than a joy. I can still see her in the kitchen, slamming cupboard doors as she resentfully made three school lunches. To this day, I flinch when a door is slammed. We didn't have much money, so the filling for these school sandwiches was sometimes just sugar or mustard or, when things were good, chopped black olives. I didn't care. I knew Dad was doing the best he could. There were periods when my dad was unemployed, but each morning he would catch the bus and pretend he was going to work so no one would know. He was a proud man, who wanted to support his family, but work wasn't always available.

During these years, my mother received large sums of money from her deceased relatives. My grandfather had nine brothers and one sister. Of the ten siblings, only one brother had children. As they died off, their considerable wealth was divided between my mother and her two sisters.

The inherited money was a valuable contribution to our family's income. On the day one of these cheques arrived, I knew it would be a good day because my mum would be overjoyed. I don't remember how many times this happened, but one of the cheques was for $25,000 and it felt like a million dollars. It was feast or famine financially—there were times when there was a lot of money and other times where there was none. I found our unpredictable money situation very unsettling. Sometimes there was money for school supplies and other times there wasn't. I never knew what was around the corner. The hypervigilance was exhausting. But when I was a young girl, it was normal.

When I was six, I entered the school system. I loved school from the first day. It brought me great joy. The smell of a new *Dick and Jane* book, the smooth feel of my notebook pages and the deep rich scent of Crayola crayons still bring up beautiful memories.

I loved the order of the school day. We would enter the school in single file like little foot soldiers and put our coats on hooks in the cloakroom. There was a place for our outside shoes underneath, and we would then put on our indoor shoes. There was a scent of wet wool, peanut butter sandwiches and lemon cleaner. There was a feeling of safety and order in the classroom. You knew where you sat and what was expected—there were no surprises.

Miss Smith was my Grade 1 teacher. At the end of each day, after all the other kids had left, I would approach her desk and wait patiently until she looked up. She was so beautiful and never got upset with me.

"Thank you for the lovely day, Miss Smith," I said, every day of Grade 1.

I now wonder what Miss Smith must have thought of me. Perhaps she thought I was a little dimwitted for saying the same thing every day, but I thought it was important for her to know the role she played in my life. She was safe, warm and always the same, day after day. She was so unlike my struggling mother. I was glad I had Miss Smith in my life.

My mum and dad spent so many hours fighting that the fighting became normal. It was sometimes over money, but often it was because they were both so unhappy in their marriage. During these fights, my mother's anger would escalate into rage and I knew to make myself scarce if I didn't want to get caught up in her wrath. I would cover my ears and find a place to hide in the crawl space in the basement. Here in my below-ground sanctuary, I would go inside myself and find the quiet. I could pretend everything was okay and spent hours creating and sharing happy stories for my three doll audience. When the shouting stopped, I would emerge knowing the worst was over. Another storm had passed.

I also had another retreat that served me well when things were chaotic at home. There was a large wooded area across the street. In the middle of the dense forest was a clearing, and in the clearing was a large rope swing anchored to a huge maple tree. It was a thick piece of rope tied at the end in an enormous knot. I would take a run at the rope, sit on the knot and soon find myself flying high above the ground. I loved the sweet scent of moist earth below my feet, the caress of the fragrant air as it swept my hair off my face and the filtered sunlight arching through the canopy of treetops. I was free and no one could touch me. I loved being alone. Back and forth I went, legs crossed, my small hands holding tight, concealed in a forest sanctuary. Then, it would be time to go home. I never knew what would greet me when I opened the door. Some days were good, but on other days, I wished I could spend the rest of my life on that rope swing.

As time passed, the girl on the swing became a teenager. Family had less influence. Friends became my world. There was a group of us that met regularly. The boys were a few years older and many of them played in a band. My best friend, Marg, and I would faithfully attend the band rehearsals and dances. Music was such an incredibly strong influence in the 1960s. We would go to parties on the weekend and dance for hours with our friends. It was a happy time, an innocent time. We smoked cigarettes but didn't drink alcohol or take drugs. We were just high on life. Whenever I hear music from that era, it never fails to take me back to those years. Songs like "Be My

Baby," "You've Lost That Lovin' Feeling" and "Hang on Sloopy" insulated me from a continuing unhappy family situation.

The connections I made in my high school years still continue to this day. Marg and I are still best friends and we enjoy remembering "the good old days." What a joy! She was always someone I could trust. Like Miss Smith from Grade 1, Marg brought a sense of continuity, predictability and great love.

CHAPTER 2

Meeting My Husband and Starting a Family

When I was eighteen, I met my husband, Greg. He was a tall, dark, handsome twenty-two-year-old from Toronto. He and his friends rented a penthouse apartment in the West End of Vancouver. Music was something we both loved. "Up On Cripple Creek" and "She Came in Through the Bathroom Window" became staples in our lives. We were married in 1969.

As with all young couples, it took time for us to find our rhythm. When I say rhythm, I mean the joining of two single lives into a married couple. In the beginning of a relationship, most often, each partner puts their best foot forward to hopefully impress the other person. It's interesting to me that, especially in the 1960s and 1970s, many of us married very young. I was only nineteen and Greg was twenty-three. I was still a teenager by definition. And yet I thought I was ready to take on the responsibility of being a wife. What did I know? It seemed like the right thing to do at the time. And in so many ways it was. But in other ways, I was very naive in my thinking. I saw my parents' marriage and knew what I didn't want. But I hadn't spent much time designing what I did want in a relationship. I thought everything would just fall into place. Yes, I was naive! I truly believed I would have the happily-ever-after Cinderella marriage.

Now looking back over fifty years, I can see things from a much different perspective. There were many good times but also many painful, challenging and demanding moments. All that truly is the nature of marriage. The challenges gave me the opportunity to finally begin to understand who I was and what I stood for in this life.

I entered marriage with the hope Greg could provide the security I lacked as a child. It was an unfair expectation because he could only do so much. It was my work, but I didn't know it at the time. It would take many years and a catastrophic event to completely break me open and help me understand my true self. I realize that, even though we walk together in our life, we're actually alone on this journey. We seek and struggle to maintain deep connections with other people. Then we worry we'll lose that lifeline either through breakup or death. If we worked that hard with the relationship with ourselves, we'd have nothing to fear because that is the connection we're really all looking for. It's the essence of the Divine that dwells in our soul. We want to be loved, to be held, to be safe. We already are, but sometimes we may doubt we can trust. So we look for others to love and hold us, make us feel safe. I have learned the responsibility lies with us. It's a continual process. Close to thirty-three years after marrying Greg, I would face the biggest challenge of my life, and I would survive! I would survive and actually thrive in a life-changing event that almost destroyed me. Spirit was preparing me for what was to come. But let's start with an introduction to Jamie, a gift from heaven given to Greg and me.

Both of us were always drawn to children. When we were first married, we would go down to a local beach, sit on the logs and watch the children play on the swings and teeter totters. In those days, no one considered adults watching children play a devious act. As the pungent salt air filled our lungs, we would consider names for our children. I wanted four, but Greg was pretty set on two. We decided if we had a boy, he would be Jamie and if it was a girl, she would be Jenny. As the waves gently rolled in and out, I thought about all the generations who may have sat on these same logs thinking about their future children. I wondered where our children were before they came to us. Are they up in heaven somewhere planning which parents they'll chose? Are they lining up on the other side of the revolving door from heaven? I like to think there's some divine plan.

My doctor said it would probably take at least three months to become pregnant because I'd been taking birth control pills since I was married. But he was wrong! I became pregnant about thirty seconds after coming off the pill. Well, certainly within a matter of days. I remember thinking, *This baby is so ready to make their presence known on earth.*

For as long as I can remember, I wanted to be a mother. When I found out I was pregnant, at the age of twenty-three, I was so elated. I loved the way the baby moved inside me.

One day, when I was sitting very still on the couch waiting for another rambunctious kick, I was aware of a vibration coming from my stomach. It wasn't exactly words, but more like the sound of a gentle wave. As I closed my eyes, the message was very distant but I picked it up. This little soul on the other side of their worldly beginning said, *"Hey Mum, it's me."* I remember thinking how incredible it was to have communication with this little person I had yet to meet.

Jamie was born, February 5, 1973. I remember getting up at 7:30 that morning and saying to Greg, "How would you like to become a father today?"

Greg spent the next hour or so trying to figure out what to wear! He didn't want to be too hot, but on the other hand, delivery rooms could be chilly, so he didn't want to be underdressed. He kept coming out of the bedroom in a variety of outfits, asking for my opinion. Finally we settled on jeans and a lovely striped blue tee shirt. I can't remember what I wore. It didn't seem too crucial as I knew I'd soon be sporting a one-size-fits-all hospital gown. I glanced down at my enormous stomach and thought about the soul packing his or her bags on the inside for one of the greatest journeys. It was a unique trip that had started nine months before somewhere beyond human understanding. My body would soon release someone who I would love in human form for the next twenty-nine years, three months, twelve days, seven hours, thirty-six minutes. He was someone who I would love in spirit form forever.

Just five short hours later, Jamie arrived. In those days, it was a novel idea to allow husbands into the delivery room. Greg, who had so carefully dressed for the occasion, was directed to don a set of pale green scrubs. He was also instructed to put on an operating room hat to cover his voluminous Afro hairstyle. He'd been blessed with his mother's strong curly hair, which tended to give him a Jethro Tull family resemblance. He was finally set, appropriately dressed to meet his son for the first time. I told him to take some deep breaths. I took a few myself.

I always love the way birth is portrayed on TV or in movies. There's usually a close-up shot of the surprised look on the mother's face when the first contraction hits. Then perhaps a few scenes of her face again, grimacing and laced with a dewy dusting of perspiration. Dad is often telling Mum how well she's doing—as if he has any idea. Then, the smiling faces as Mum and Dad hold the new infant tenderly between them. Well, as any of you mothers know, there's a great deal more to the story than that! For those of you who are not mothers, it might be a good idea to skip to the next few paragraphs.

Birth involves pain beyond any descriptive word found in Webster's Dictionary. It briefly went through my mind that perhaps I'd somehow forgotten to read the fine print of the baby delivery agreement. I didn't remember giving permission for both my legs and hands to be strapped down—in those days, it was common practice. I don't remember the warnings about possible incontinence of stool and multiple haemorrhoids the size of Chilean grapes clusters appearing unexpectedly during a particularly vigorous marathon of bearing down. And, oh yes, did the baby delivery agreement prepare me for the river of bloody fluid streaming off the delivery table onto the floor? Hmm, don't remember that part being highlighted. Just as all this was coming together like the crescendo in a well-orchestrated symphony, the conductor—my doctor—asked me if I would like to look at myself in the mirror. He was not offering up a facial view. He was inviting me to view, in Kodak technicolour, the events taking place between my legs.

It was excellent timing. From the most intimate private place of my body, a battlefield of pain, blood and Chilean grape clusters, emerged a tiny head. A short time later, Jamie worked himself from the depths of my body into the spotlight created by the overhead lights. The whole cast of characters in the delivery room drama clapped and cried, including the doctor and both nurses. Never in my twenty-three years of living had I felt such profound happiness.

His beautiful little toes would carry the weight of his body for his lifetime. His hands would learn to peel an orange, strum a guitar and twenty-nine years later hold his baby daughter, Taylor May. He would touch the hearts of many people. But in that moment, he had nothing to do but start his human experience.

CHAPTER 3

Raising a Family and Finding My Passion

Jamie was a child full of wonder. He seemed to be in awe of everything he saw. I remember the day we planted an apple tree. He was about four. I dug the hole and when the tree was in place, he watered the roots with his little yellow watering can. The next spring, he was curious to see the blossoms appear. When the apples began to form, he was amazed to see what this tree could do. He would take time to examine each perfect little apple and asked many questions about how the tree knew to make these perfect pieces of fruit. His first taste of the apples brought a big grin to his sweet little face. He was truly enamoured of the wisdom of nature.

The next few years brought many challenges. As with most marriages, cracks sometimes develop as husbands and wives learn to live together. By this time, the cracks in my mother and father's marriage had become deep craters. My mother had found yet another boyfriend and eagerly shared her experiences with me whenever she could. My father was heartbroken and frequently sat at my dining room table in tears, head down. I found myself in the middle of their chaos. I began having panic attacks.

Agoraphobia is a type of anxiety disorder in which you fear and avoid places or situations that might cause you to panic or feel trapped, helpless or embarrassed. Panic attacks are a symptom of agoraphobia, but they're not exclusive to it. I was overwhelmed with stress. I had a young child and challenges in my own marriage, and I was trying be the kind of daughter I thought I should be for my parents. The attacks were frightening. My heart would pound, my mouth would become dry and I would have a hard time breathing. If I experienced an episode in a grocery store, I would avoid going there in case it happened again. If I was in an elevator, the next time, I found I had to take the stairs. If I was driving, I lived in fear it would surface again the next time I had to go somewhere. So I stopped driving anywhere. I stayed home most of the time. I was held prisoner by my anxiety.

I now know stress finds a way out of the body. It's like a pressure cooker. If the valve on the top is blocked, the pressure builds, until eventually the top blows off. Panic attacks are a similar feeling. You think you're dying. And in a way, you are.

It took me two years to find the strength to conquer these attacks. I wanted another child and I knew I couldn't until a solution was found. So I worked hard at changing my inner dialogue. I tried to stop worrying so much and slowly the panic attacks stopped. It was such a relief. I promised myself I would never allow my stress levels to consume me again. And they never have. I began a lifelong practice of meditation. It has been and continues to be one of my greatest tools. I also began learning more about spiritual matters. It's a good thing I was learning because the challenges in my life were only just beginning.

It was during this time, I experienced the first of many spiritual connections with the other side. The birth of Jamie was the first concrete spiritual experience I remember. He came from somewhere across the sea of forever and became my son. It was truly profound. Birth happens every day, but it was different when it happened to me. I thought it was a miracle.

A man named Bert was the next confirmation something existed beyond the reality of this world.

We lived beside an older couple, Bert and Alberte. Jamie was two years old, and he loved going next door to visit. They always welcomed him in and fed him endless cookies. They became his surrogate grandparents.

Bert was a spry seventy-year-old Scotsman who lived with his French Canadian wife, Alberte. They had only been married to each other for two months when my husband and I moved in and became neighbours. They were like newlyweds, always together.

A small man, Bert rather resembled a ceramic elf you might see in a formal garden, perhaps by a fountain or peeking out from behind the rose bushes. He reminded me of my favourite character, Doc, in the fairytale Snow White.

He was an avid gardener. From my kitchen window, I would hear him whistling as he worked in his vegetable garden. He and I would spend hours in his backyard, drinking countless cups of coffee and discussing the merits of organic gardening. Even though his doctor had warned Bert about the hazards of smoking, his package of Number 7s was never far from reach. Consumption of alcoholic beverages was also on the forbidden list. But that didn't stop him from sneaking out to his workshop for a "wee quick one" when Alberte wasn't looking. He had his own private party, but he wasn't completely alone. He had a constant companion—pain.

Bert had a serious heart condition, one that demanded countless operations. The arteries from various parts of his body were used to replace the damaged ones to his heart. His chest resembled an intricate road map. The red twisting roads were grotesque scar tissue from many incisions. His body had betrayed him, but his spirit was strong.

Although his legs were crippled and he required a cane to walk, he was forever dancing Alberte around their living room. Sometimes he would show me little Scottish jigs he'd mastered as a child. He would accompany himself with songs so heavy with Gaelic accent it was difficult to understand the words.

As time passed, the pain became more intense. He was like a wounded bird, hobbling around with the aid of his cane. Sitting in my backyard, I would smell the sweet pungent smoke from his pipe, the air alive with visions of autumn bonfires. Looking over the fence I would see him sitting at his picnic table. His face would be contorted with pain and tears. It was so unfair! He never knew I saw him; he didn't want my pity.

Even though he wasn't related, Bert was like family to all of us. He would spend hours with Jamie, singing his Scottish songs and doing tricks. Jamie's favourite was when Bert would smile, dropping his upper denture with a clicking sound. His face would resemble a mechanical clown's face, with the big red nose, gaping smile and wide open eyes. Always a laugh, always a joke, always the pain.

One Christmas morning, Bert knocked on my back door as I was finishing my breakfast. He had a bottle of Canadian Club in his hand. I'll never forget the taste of scrambled eggs and Canadian Club. It was not a pleasant experience, but I knew it was important to him. He reached out with his gnarled old hand and covered mine. His touch conveyed all the love and caring that a thousand words could not say. I looked at him and in his eyes I saw what we both knew was true.

Bert died three days later. The battle was over and his body had won.

He had requested a memorial service, thoughtful right to the end. After the service, we joined Alberte and her family next door. The house was so empty without Bert. The stale smell of pipe smoke lingered. His package of Number 7s sat on the dining room table. His slippers were neatly together by the front door where he always left them.

"Bert," I called in a whisper, "please don't leave me yet. Please come back and we'll pretend it's all a bad dream."

The house looked the same; I couldn't believe he was gone. It was my first brush with death and I couldn't accept the finality of it. Alberte, along with her family, went out into the garden. I needed a couple of minutes to myself.

As I began to walk home, I looked over our adjoining fence and that's when I saw him. Bert was sitting on Jamie's sandbox in the far corner of our yard. He was smoking his pipe, legs crossed, and resting his chin on his hand, as if he was contemplating the gathering in his own back garden. I closed my eyes for a moment. I could almost smell the smoke from his pipe.

"Bert, you didn't leave me after all," I whispered. I opened my eyes. I could see through him. His eyes met mine, and I wasn't afraid. He slowly faded away like fog clearing in the presence of sunlight.

I never said anything to anyone. It was between Bert and me. Afterwards I continued on home. I needed to be alone.

As I lay on my bed, eyes closed, I was aware of a presence in the room. When I opened my eyes, I found myself alone. But I could feel something touch me, not just in one spot, but all over my body at one time. It seemed to envelope me, almost a vapour or a mist. It was a comforting feeling, as if warm water had been poured over me. Bert wanted to come, to comfort me, but I was afraid. He must have sensed my feelings. He left as he had come and I was alone again. I felt a sadness, but at the same time, an acceptance.

The most important part of Bert, his spirit, had survived. Death hadn't won!

I see Bert each time I see another person struggling. I see him in sick people—the human spirit. Trying to describe it is like trying to put the emotion of love on paper, trying to hold a snowflake or trying to explain the feeling of peace. It's what uniquely makes you "you," the part that lives and knows.

The event with Bert was a little frightening for me. When I saw him sitting on Jamie's sandbox, the image seemed unreal. But it was real. I'm no longer afraid when unusual things happen in my life. I don't have a need to always understand. Things happen as they need to happen. I didn't know it at the time, but Bert would be the first of a lifelong parade of departed souls who would connect with me. He was the beautiful lead spirit and paved the way for others to infiltrate my life.

My second son, Sean, sauntered into my life ten months later. I say sauntered because that's exactly what it felt like. His birth, from start to finish, was a mere three hours. He was a placid baby; he seemed just happy to be here. He was content with life and rewarded us with frequent smiles and laughter. He never got too upset if other children took his toys. He'd just turn to another truck or puzzle. This calm approach to life became a lifelong strength for Sean. Life was good.

While my children were young, I was lucky to have the option of staying home instead of working. It was an era when one pay cheque seemed to adequately cover the needs of a growing family. I loved those years. I was able to absorb every day as my two sons learned to walk, talk and feed themselves. Jamie was delighted to have a baby brother. I have pictures of him sitting in his little rocking chair with Sean in the carriage beside him. He would read to him for hours from *The Story of Ferdinand, MacGooses' Grocery,* and *Sam Sunday and the Strange Disappearance of Chester Cats.* His favourite was about Ferdinand the bull.

He would start with "There was a little bull and his name was Ferdinand. All the other little bulls he lived with would run and jump and butt their heads together, but not Ferdinand." His voice would rise when he said, "not Ferdinand."

Sean always smiled at this. Jamie couldn't actually read because he was only four, but he knew the stories so well he could tell by the pictures what the words said. The brothers were always together. It was like they had known each other for lifetimes. There was a special bond right from the beginning.

The problems with my parents continued. They lived together, but they were miserable. It was a very unhappy time for our family. I often thought it would have been better if they had separated early. It was as if they were slowly and painfully pulling off an old band-aid, ripping the skin of their love with it. When Greg was given an opportunity to work in Vernon, we jumped at the chance. In 1977, we sold our house and left Vancouver. It was easier to deal with my parents when there was distance between us.

Within a short period of time, however, one by one, my family also decided to move to Vernon. First my brother, Pete, moved there. Then came my sister and her three children, Polly, Michelle and Tyler. Then my mum moved, followed shortly by my father. So we were all, once again, living in the same city. And life continued.

When Jamie started Kindergarten, the school bus would pick him up each morning and drop him off in the afternoon at the end of the street. Sean would station himself at the window as soon as he woke up from his afternoon nap.

He would patiently wait until he could see the bright yellow bus with its flashing lights. Then he'd jump up and start shouting, "Jamie's home! Jamie's home!" It was the highlight of his day to be reunited with his brother. I can still see them in the middle of the living room surrounded by mountains of brightly coloured Lego, chatting away as they constructed yet another masterpiece. They were brothers in arms.

In 1985, Greg became the manager of an electrical company in Kamloops. Sean was eight and Jamie was twelve. This move was hard, much harder than our previous move to Vernon.

I suppose, in some ways, I ran from my problems when we left Vancouver. The unhappy situation with my parents' marriage had begun to consume me. I wanted to find a solution to their problems, but my marriage was still so new. I didn't have much experience living with my own husband. How could I possibly help my mum and dad?

When the move to Kamloops came along, I had learned I couldn't fix anybody else, only myself. It took me many years to finally see how children can take on the role of the parent and think they need to solve the other's problems. I had found a way to live in the same city as my parents and not get as involved with their struggles. I loved being close to my sister and brother. I didn't want to move, but move we did. Little did I know, this move would spin my life in a brand new direction, beyond my wildest dreams.

Once the relocation took place, I decided I needed to do something. The boys seemed to be handling the move well. They had started school and were making friends. I, on the other hand, didn't have a focus and found myself missing my family in Vernon. I felt myself becoming depressed, so I visited my local college. I thought I might look into social work. The counsellor I spoke to asked me if I had ever considered nursing as a career. Although my grandfather had been a doctor, and my grandmother along with two of my aunts had been nurses, I never thought I was smart enough to be a nurse. But it intrigued me and I went home to discuss the idea with Greg and the boys. I didn't have the high school credits to enter the nursing program. I would have to upgrade my Grade 11 and 12 subjects so I could qualify to apply to the School of Nursing. It was somewhat humiliating, at thirty-six years old, to register in classes full of seventeen- and eighteen-year-olds. But there was only one way to move forward and that was to swallow my pride and just do it.

I believe there are major crossroads in our lives. We don't always see the significance until years later. My decision to become a nurse was one of those crossroads for me. From a challenging situation—moving to Kamloops— came an amazing gift. I was able to recognize and pursue what I now know was my soul's work.

I finished my upgrade and was accepted into nursing. During the following three years, I learned so much about life in general. I felt like I had found my way home. The years with Sean and Jamie had been rewarding, but I knew they were past needing me to greet them at the door with milk and cookies. If they were to grow into healthy young men, I needed to create my own life so they could live theirs. I had witnessed too many mothers hanging on to their grown sons as if they were still little boys.

The rigour of school provided a needed challenge for me. It reminded me of my younger days in school. I enjoyed the learning, the writing, the precise nature of things, like the sterile procedure. It's interesting how, if you listen carefully enough, your true nature finds a voice. Becoming a nurse was a pivotal point in my life and helped prepare me for what was to come.

From the moment I walked into my first class until graduation, I loved every moment. Nursing fit me to a tee. The theory classes were so interesting. I was fascinated with how the human body worked. The clinical side was equally satisfying. Caring for others had been at the centre of my life for many years. Now it became my life's work.

Early in my clinical rotation at the hospital, I found myself drawn to those who were dying. One woman in particular stands out in my mind.

When I walked into the hospital room, she looked so small sitting on her bed, a quilt tucked around her.

"I'm close to home now," she said. She turned her head to look at me. "Is this the end?"

"What do you think?" I asked gently.

She nodded. "Yes, this is the end." She seemed relieved, being able to verbalize what she felt. "Thank you for listening to me."

I remember thinking what a privilege it was to be included in such an intimate conversation with a complete stranger. Even back then, I knew I wanted to pursue end-of-life care. It seemed death was something we didn't talk enough about until it happened to us.

In the hospital, when someone dies, we tend to hide the fact from other patients on the ward. I never quite understood this. It's like there's some sort of shame in dying, a failure somehow. When nurses transport a body to the morgue in the basement, we try to camouflage what we're doing by covering the body with a metal frame to hide the outline of the human form. It made me question how society views death and dying. Even early in my career, I was wanting to understand more about death and issues surrounding it. This interest continues to be an ongoing theme in my life to this day.

I now know I'm an empath, someone who is acutely aware of others' feelings and emotions. This trait served me well as a student nurse. I was able to trust my intuition about patients. This helped me to address not only the physical needs of individuals in my care, but their emotional and spiritual needs as well. I began to understand the sensitivity I'd developed as a child had prepared me in so many ways to do this work. Again I saw how something that I'd deemed negative had blossomed into a treasured positive. It was second nature. Nursing fit like a glove.

After one year of upgrading and three years of further education, at the age of forty, I became a registered nurse. It was such a proud day for me. All my family came to the graduation. I was valedictorian for the class of 1989.

My dear mother was a proud peacock that day. She strutted around, saying, "I'm the valedictorian's mother!" to anyone who would listen. I was so embarrassed.

Graduation day was a Saturday and I started working at the local hospital on the following Monday. Literally overnight, I went from a student nurse to a registered nurse. The responsibility took my breath away, but I couldn't wait to begin my career. The first few years flew by and it wasn't long before I felt the craving for more education.

In the early '90s there was a shortage of critical care nurses in the province. I decided to take the additional courses and clinical education to be able to work in the critical care unit at our hospital. I loved learning about heart rhythms and cardiac drugs. I went to Vancouver to complete the hands-on portion of my education. A position came up in neurological intensive care. It was a six-bed unit that cared for patients undergoing brain surgery, along with patients with brain injury, strokes and a variety of neurological conditions. As nurses, we were also involved in organ-retrieval work. I enjoyed the challenge of this new position. The work was complicated and often emotionally draining, but I thrived on its complexity.

There was a period of time where there were multiple donors, most of them young. Some had been injured in car accidents. Some of them died from aneurysms, a weakening of one of the vessels in the brain, which causes bleeding inside the brain. It can be fatal because the brain is encased in the skull, and when the aneurysm bursts, there's no space for the blood. These children were all eventually declared "brain dead," which meant their brains were so damaged, they wouldn't survive without the life-sustaining machines that were keeping them alive. I watched as mothers and fathers and siblings said goodbye. I couldn't imagine the pain they must be feeling. As I witnessed the last words family members exchanged, I felt such overwhelming sadness.

This was not the natural order of things. I cried as I witnessed the most primal anguish of a mother watching life drain out of her child. Little did I know, I too would be faced with the same challenge in my life.

There had been so many young people who had died in a few short months. This was a breaking point for me. I began to burn out. As much as I wanted to keep working in this unit, I knew I had to find different work because my heart couldn't witness another child dying. I needed to leave and I transferred out the next week. I have never regretted making that decision. Again, it was a crossroad in my life. I listened to my inner wisdom and made a change. I wanted to find something positive that would give birth to the next part of my life journey. I didn't have to wait long for this to happen—I took a position back on the neurology ward and began working with student nurses. I found I enjoyed mentoring students and it opened another world for me.

About this time, I had an experience that created a thread in my life's journey, one I would not recognize until years later. Looking back I can see how the pieces of my life fit together like a jigsaw puzzle. But at the time the incident happened, I couldn't see how it fit.

It was 1995. We had eight very large pine trees growing in the ravine behind our house. They had to be close to a hundred years old. I often sat on my deck and drank in the beauty of these majestic pioneer trees. I learned to unfocus my eyes so I could see the luminescent energy flowing around each one. I could almost hear them breathe. Sometimes, especially at dusk, I would climb down the cement steps and join them at the bottom of the ravine. It was a magical time. It reminded me of being on the rope swing as a child. I found healing and comfort being near the trees. I would hug the trunk of one of the trees and put my ear up to the fragrant bark to hear the faint pulse of the giant pine. It seemed to connect me to the earth in a way I didn't understand until I listened carefully.

One night while I was sitting on our cedar deck, a gentle wind came up. The branches on the pine trees began to rhythmically sway to the music of the breeze. After a few minutes I heard them say, "Will you stay if Jamie has to leave this earth?"

At first, I couldn't believe what I was hearing. Then the trees whispered again, "Will you stay if Jamie has to leave this earth?"

What kind of question is that? I thought. *This is ridiculous! I won't be a part of this conversation. How absurd! I must be imagining this.*

I got up out of my deck chair and went into the house. The next evening I went outside again. It was a beautiful spring evening. I could smell the fragrant purple lilacs from the next-door neighbours' yard. I could hear the shrill voices of young children playing outside after dinner. It was almost dark. The distant hills were painted with the colours of dusk to create an ebb and flow of light and shadow. I loved this time of night.

I settled into my comfortable cushioned deck chair and enjoyed the beauty of my backyard. Again the pine trees began.

"Will you stay if Jamie has to leave this earth?"

"No," I replied in my head. "I will never acknowledge your question. It doesn't even deserve an answer."

But I couldn't move from my chair. An invisible force pressed against my chest holding me in place. It waited for my answer.

I started to cry. "Let me go!" I pleaded.

Still, I could not move. It was so profoundly sad.

My soul's voice gently guided me by saying, "You know you have to listen. This is all part of what you agreed to before you came to earth. In your heart, you recognize the truth in this. Surrender."

I put my hands over my face. My heart broke and I said, "Yes, I will stay."

The moment I uttered these words, the whole conversation was erased from my mind. I was not conscious of this at the time, but years later I would revisit that backyard exchange and understand why it had to happen.

I'm not sure if things like this happen to other people. I'm sure they must, but no one talks about it. We may store things away because we're not really sure they happened. On some level, we can't deny the event. It seems real. We lived it, but it may be tidied up and stored in the shadows of our being until the perfect moment presents itself for remembrance. In some ways these experiences are surreal, like a dream. Sometimes we remember our dreams and other times they're gone from memory as soon as we wake up. The question from the trees was like that for me. I forgot about it as soon as it happened. And my life went on.

Over the next few years, I applied at the local college to teach part time as a clinical instructor. It was the best of both worlds. I worked part time as a ward nurse and was able to bring my nursing students onto the ward as an instructor. I loved it! I'd worked hard to become an accomplished neurology nurse and now I had the opportunity to teach what I loved to do. The students' curiosity and dedication brought me great pleasure. It was satisfying to explore the world of nursing through the eyes of my students. There were many times when I was aware this was again truly my soul's work. It felt so right.

The dichotomy of being a nurse and a teacher was a beautiful cross play that led me to yet another crossroad. I decided to go back to school to achieve a Bachelor of Science in Nursing. Again my passion for learning was at the centre of my life. I could almost feel like I had been here before in a former life. The books, the classes, the writing were second nature. My mind processed the knowledge as a starved animal greedily bites and chews its prey. I couldn't get enough.

After receiving my degree, along came the opportunity to apply for a newly developed position—patient care coordinator. It was a leadership role much like the head nurse of the past. I felt like this was so perfect it had to be right. I meditated many times to feel the energy of the job and each time I came away with the feeling it was the right thing to do. I was definitely stepping out of my comfort zone. I didn't have much leadership training. I was a quiet, private person. I knew I was a good nurse, but I never saw myself as a leader. I was being led by the quiet voice inside me.

I was successful in securing the position. I grew as a person and as a nurse and discovered a job I loved. The "coordination" piece of the position involved working closely with physicians, physical therapy, pharmacy, home support and various other departments. It involved coordinating a thirty-seven-bed ward. Every day brought new challenges and situations.

It was a time when hospitals were downsizing the number of beds available for patient care. The situation reminded me of the game musical chairs. Patients would figuratively line up around the hospital and hope, when the music stopped, they'd have a bed. In the late 1990s, our local hospital closed many beds. Patients who were lucky enough to be admitted grew progressively sicker. Those who would have, in the past, gone to close observation areas, were now being admitted to the medical and surgical units. Sometimes the patient load on a unit would reach overwhelming levels. The number of patients each nurse was responsible for may not have changed, but the severity and level of attention rose, making the workload extremely challenging, especially for novice nurses.

This was also the time when patients began to be housed in the hallways, sometimes with privacy screens and often without. We would refer to "over census" numbers. In other words, the capacity might be thirty-seven patients, but there were actually forty or forty-one patients on the ward. It was the beginning of the era of the health care crisis we see today—too many sick people and not enough beds. The pressure to give quality nursing care quickly escalated, and the frustration was evident on the faces of both the patients and the nurses.

During my years working at the hospital, my sons grew from teenagers into young men. They both graduated from high school and soon left home to begin their independent lives. Sean married in 2000. His wife, Lisa, was a beautiful woman who stole my heart right from the beginning. Jamie began dating a lovely girl, Lindsay. Jamie and Lindsay created a family with the birth of their daughter, Taylor, on February 12, 2002.

I will never forget seeing Jamie right after Taylor's birth. He walked out of the delivery room and into the hallway where Greg and I were waiting.

Tears streaming down his face, he said, "Mum, this is the happiest day of my life. I have a daughter."

As I hugged him, I remembered the joy I felt seeing him for the first time twenty-nine years ago.

I smile when I think of him driving Lindsay and Taylor home from the hospital. He drove very slowly and had his hazard lights flashing. My son had been transformed into a cautious person right before my eyes.

From day one, Jamie loved the role of father. Whenever I saw him, Taylor was in his arms. It was as if he couldn't get enough of her. Even when he dozed in his chair, he had Taylor sleeping on his chest. Life was so good for all of us.

In March of 2002, the hospital informed us our floor was closing in an attempt to again downsize the number of beds in the hospital. The staff was devastated and so was I. We had worked together for so many years. We had developed a closeness as a ward and now we would all go our separate ways.

A certain culture develops on a nursing unit. It can be healthy and supportive or it can carry a more negative quality. On our unit, the senior nurses took time to work with the junior ones. This is the way it should be. Learning to be an effective nurse takes time. Students come out of school with a certain degree of knowledge and practical experience, but there's still work to do learning to carry the responsibility of a complex ever-changing work environment. New nurses should never feel alone when they begin their careers. The support of senior nurses is crucial in the early months and years. I worked hard to mentor when I could. Sometimes it was just a second opinion of a patient status. Other times, it would be a family situation or a new experience as a patient died. It was reassuring to talk to others when struggles surfaced, and they did on a regular basis.

As April turned into May, I began making plans for how the ward would close. The hardest part of my life was about to unfold in less than three weeks.

Part Two:
The Catastrophe

CHAPTER 4

The Loss of My Son

I never saw it coming. On May 18, 2002, Jamie was instantly killed in a motor vehicle accident at the age of twenty-nine.

It was the May long weekend. Greg and I had recently bought a trailer and parked it out in the Shuswap at Pine Grove next to the Provincial Park. It was only a few miles from Chase. Greg had gone out early Friday. I had to work but drove out Friday night. At 6:00 Saturday morning, when I woke up, I received an inner message that told me to go home. I was used to receiving messages. I think of them as inner knowings, understandings. So I packed up and left for home. Greg was used to my "ways" and didn't question my need to go.

When I got home, I received another message from Spirit. I was told to get into my nightgown and get into bed. I remember thinking how odd that was. I had only just got up, but I did what I was instructed to do. I felt like I was in a dream state. Nothing made sense but I intuitively knew I had to listen.

I slept from 8:00 a.m. until 10:00 a.m. I awoke to the telephone ringing. It was Lindsay. She was upset because she couldn't reach Jamie on his cell phone. I didn't know, but Jamie had travelled out to the Shuswap the previous night to attend a birthday party. Lindsay was worried because she had heard about an accident outside of Chase. She said there was a compact car involved and she wondered if Jamie's Honda would be considered a compact. I told her not to worry and that I would be over to see her shortly. I walked into my bedroom and bumped into an invisible denseness. This is the best way I can describe what I felt. It stopped me in my tracks. I couldn't see it, but I could feel it. I remember saying out loud, "No, no, no!" My conscious mind didn't want to look at what my subconscious wisdom knew to be the truth. I realized later Jamie had been in the room in his new spirit form. I had slept while he died.

In the meantime, Greg drove the road from the trailer to Chase, about twenty-eight kilometres. He needed to go to the hardware store.

Shortly before 8:00 a.m., Jamie called Greg on his cell. Jamie said he was on his way home and wanted to bring Lindsay and Taylor out later that day for a visit. He said he was just coming into Chase and would call him later.

At 8:10 a.m., Jamie crossed the centre line and hit a motorhome that was pulling a trailer with two ATVs. The couple in the motorhome said it appeared Jamie looked down to his right, perhaps to answer a page or his phone. The Honda slid under the other vehicle, was pushed off the road and instantly burst into flames. On a beautiful sunny Saturday morning, my son Jamie died.

As Greg approached the scene of the accident, the cars were lined up for miles. He had a terrible feeling that Jamie was involved in this accident. Greg parked his truck and started walking.

When he reached the first police officer, he asked, "What kind of car is under there?" gesturing to the motorhome.

The officer shook his head. "It's so badly damaged it's impossible to tell."

"Can I take a closer look?" With building dread, he stepped up onto the train tracks that ran alongside the highway. When he saw the distinct hubcaps of Jamie's Honda, he fell to his knees—he knew for sure it was his son. Two policemen began walking towards him; they had confirmed the licence plate number.

Greg had been there, Afro hair and all, at Jamie's birth and saw him take his first breath. He was there shortly after Jamie took his last breath and watched his firstborn son leave the earth in a surge of flames. The images of that day in May are tattooed on his soul. My heart aches when I think of him alone at the side of the road, feeling such incomprehensible pain. It was hard for all of us, but Greg paid the highest price by witnessing the scene of the accident.

Two critical incident workers were called to help Greg. One drove his truck and the other transported him back to Kamloops.

Meanwhile, Lindsay had phoned Sean and he agreed to leave his home and drive the highway to see if something had happened to Jamie. He, too, came upon the long line of cars. He also approached the police to ask about the accident.

"What's your name?" a female officer asked him.

"Sean Ross."

"You had better come with me." She added, "It's your brother."

I cannot imagine the anguish Sean must have felt as he witnessed the carnage of his brother's vehicle.

As they drove to Kamloops, Sean asked about Jamie's injuries.

The officer reached over and put her hand on his knee. "I'm sorry. He's gone." The brother who had walked every mile of Sean's life with him was no longer alive.

As with Greg, Sean was alone when he found out Jamie was dead and he also witnessed the scene of the accident. I often hear people say there's a reason for everything. The three men in my life came together that day in the most painful way imaginable and somehow I was spared by that early morning message that told me to go home.

The cars carrying Greg and Sean met on the highway outside of Kamloops. Both men got out and hugged each other for a long time. Sean left the police car and joined Greg in the car driven by the critical incident worker. Together they made the last leg of the journey into town. Sean later told me he doesn't have much memory of the accident scene. The mind can be such an advocate for us when we need it to be.

By this time, I had joined Lindsay and Taylor at their home. Together we sat on her bed and listened to the news on the radio; we were hoping for details that showed it was impossible for Jamie to be involved in the accident. Then I heard Lindsay's mum at the door talking to someone.

"It's not Jamie, is it? It's not Jamie?" and then, "Oh my God, oh my God! It's Jamie!" Sean and Greg were walking up the driveway as she said this.

NO ... NO ... NO! Not my son!! Dead! How could that be? I just saw him on Mother's Day. Dead! No, no, no. There must be some mistake. Where are you, God? Do you have him? Where is he? You gave him to me twenty-nine years ago. Now give him back!!!

Can't be true! Not my child with the crooked smile and the perfect little toes and fingers, lost in a fiery crash ... no, no, take me instead! This can't be true ... not my child, not my child—

It was my child and he was dead.

There are no words to express the depth of grief we experienced that day. Greg went into the house to be with Lindsay. Sean and I sat on the front steps. I felt remarkably calm. It was like I was in a bubble.

I remember Sean saying, "Mum, there's nowhere to hide. The work begins now."

Sean took such care with me that day. He didn't talk very much, which was just what I needed. It was as if he put his own grief on the back burner and focused on me. I will always be grateful to him for his beautiful calm presence.

The hours following Jamie's death felt like time was standing still. My mind was racing.

How could this possibly be happening? Not to my son. Not my son. Not my son. Not to my son. Where is he? This can't be right. We're all here together—our family. Where is Jamie? He should be here, just like he always is. He's always here. Will he walk up the driveway soon? Of course he will. He always does. It's such a beautiful sunny day. Things like dying don't happen on sunny days in May. Maybe I didn't hear right. This isn't happening. He must just be late getting home. That's it. Traffic on the highway. This is my son. Terrible things don't happen in our family. He'll be home. He always comes home. Jamie, please come home—

My thoughts were interrupted by Bev, the critical incident worker. I went in the house with her.

"Who do you want to phone?" she asked.

I looked at her and wondered why she was asking that question. Then I remembered. Jamie wasn't coming home because he'd been killed that morning. She helped me dial my brother Pete's number. When he answered, I started to cry. I didn't want to say the words. It would make them true.

Finally I said, "Jamie is gone. He was killed in a car accident."

There was silence on the other end of the line. Then Pete started to cry. His ordinary Saturday had suddenly been turned upside down.

I called my sister. I don't really remember much about the conversation. By this time, I felt like I had been wrapped in cotton batten. Voices were muffled and distant.

> *One breath in, one breath out. Where's Jamie? Why isn't he here? Oh my God, he's dead … one breath in, one breath out. Who's crying? I can hear a baby crying! Someone should help that baby. Is it Jamie crying? I should help him … I'm his mother! Where is he?*

It was Taylor crying.

I went into her room and changed her diaper. She looked up at me and then her gaze focused over my right shoulder. Suddenly her little face lit up and she smiled. I could feel a presence behind me. Was Jamie that close? Was he home? Could I turn around and see him? Maybe it's not true. I started to cry again. It was true.

Elizabeth Kübler-Ross[2] was a pioneer in the area of grief theory. She developed a model of five stages of grief: denial, anger, bargaining, depression and acceptance. These stages may happen in order, but most often it's not a linear process. In the beginning, I was in denial. My brain was struggling with the truth of the situation. I wanted to bargain with God. Just let me go back before today and I will promise anything. Depression, anger and finally acceptance would trail behind as the weeks unfolded.

Bev came into the room and suggested we walk outside on the sidewalk. I was like a zombie. I let her take my hand like a child and lead me outside into the sunshine. We crossed the street and began walking down the sidewalk. The sidewalk where I had walked so many times with Jamie. The sidewalk where he pushed Taylor's buggy and took Georgia, their dog, for a walk. I don't remember much about the walk, but I do know moving my feet helped to calm me down. I walked and I cried. I cried and I walked. I wanted to just

---

[2] Elisabeth Kübler-Ross, *On death and dying* (New York: Macmillan, 1969).

curl up in the corner of someone's yard, but Bev had a firm hold of my waist and she kept saying, "You're going to be okay, just one foot in front of the other." I just wanted to lie down on the warm cement and leave this world. There was no back door to escape. I had to live through the day.

Lisa, Sean's wife, arrived a short time later and together we all went home.

As we drove, I thought, *How is the world still turning? These people we're passing all seem to be having a normal day. Don't they know? The greatest tragedy just happened. My son is dead. How can you all be so normal? How can you just go on with your day? Don't you know?*

I was full of anger. I thought back to the early morning as I drove home from the lake. Was it only this morning? I was normal. I'm not normal anymore and I never will be again.

That night, long after Greg and I had gone to bed, Sean and Lisa heard a strange noise coming from the basement of our home. They mentioned it the next morning. I went downstairs and opened the closet door in the room that had once been Jamie's bedroom.

I could hear Sean saying upstairs, "That's the noise we heard last night."

When I got back upstairs, we all looked at each other and something unspoken passed between us. Little did we know this was only the beginning of Jamie's communication with his family.

The first few days, I did nothing but cry. I screamed at God from the private confines of my car while driving on the highway. The raw primal sound of my screams rocked me to my very foundation. I wanted to pretend my son with the loving blue eyes would walk into my house again. I found myself stumbling around in the darkness of my grief. There were no signposts to guide me. How could I accept the reality? I didn't know how to do this. I didn't want to do this.

The next few days I focused on breathing in and breathing out. It was about all I could concentrate on doing. Many people came to the door and we would sit in the living room and cry together. I remember, in particular, a group of Jamie's friends coming to see us. They sat and just looked at me. It was as if they were hoping I would have some answers for them, some form of comfort. But I had nothing to give anyone.

It was impossible to eat, sleep, concentrate. I told Greg I had to go to the accident site. I had to see for myself. Fortunately he agreed to drive me. I say "fortunately" because I would have walked the fifty kilometres to the scene of the accident if I had to. It was so important to see where it happened. Since that time, I have done a great deal of reading on this very thing. Many people need to see where their loved one died. It is part of the acceptance that the brain needs to really believe the death has happened. The accident was on a straight stretch of highway.

Both the motorhome and Jamie's car ended up off the side of the road. The grass was blackened and there were small pieces of things hidden in the blades. I went through each bit of debris. I wasn't sure what I was looking for, but I just knew I had to do it. There were pieces of metal and objects I couldn't identify. Already there was a small cross and a small pile of rocks set up in his memory. Various little items had been left along with some food. Hung on the cross was a small wind chime. It was comforting to see these things but at the same time, I felt horror that these small items were all that was left of my son.

There were messages from others who had visited the site. There were people who cared enough to drive out to Chase to pay respects to Jamie. We left after a few minutes. I was so thankful Greg was able to go with me. It must have been so hard for him to revisit the place where he had suffered so much a few days before. I have to be honest. At the time, I didn't think of this. All I knew was that I needed to touch the place where Jamie took his last breath.

Days were spent crying, feeling the pain. I rejected the suggestion of medication for the grief and anxiety. I knew I had to feel it. There was no escape. I would not hide.

CHAPTER 5

The Journal Years

I once again turned inward, using my meditation to help me find answers. Within the deep, dark state of my subconscious, I found a thread of relief. I could suspend the reality of Jamie's death and float in a calm sea of nothingness. There was no pain, no thought, no noise … just the beating of my heart and a sense of surrender. Then I heard it, like a dull foghorn in dense fog. It seemed to come from a distance like a weak signal across a sea of forever. The vibration became faint words. *"Hey Mum, it's me."*

My mind wrestled with this unseen possibility. Could it be?

"Jamie," I called back in a language without words.

And then it began. I call it a "transmission" because that's the only way I can explain the connection I had with my son. There were no words exchanged and yet there was understanding. His words took form and I began to write. It was during these first few days that the communication with Jamie became very strong. It was almost as if he was trying to help us endure this painful time. Sometimes the words would come so quickly I could hardly write fast enough to keep up. Other times, the messages came in the form of a picture or a symbol. They would come, at first, only in meditation. But as time went on, they would come no matter where I was.

I have since learned there's a word for what happened to me: "idionecrophany." It's the experience of perceiving contact with the dead.[3] It most often

---

[3] William MacDonald, "Idionecrophanies: the social construction of perceived contact with the dead," *Journal for the Scientific Study of Religion* 31, no. 2 (June 1, 1992): 215–223.

appears in females because women tend to invest in relationships with others and are more open to intuition and emotion as real forms of knowledge. They tend to maintain bonds with the deceased. Men may see idionecrophanies as irrational and have difficulty believing they can happen.

I began to journal these exchanges and they became a map as my life moved forward. A few days after Jamie's accident, I was sitting in my living room and looked out the window. I saw animal faces in the pine trees. There was the face of a bear, deer, elk and tiger. The images faded in and out of focus. I understood that Jamie wanted to show me what he was seeing. The animals were so beautiful. He also sent a message telling me about the amazing colours, like nothing he'd ever seen on earth. He said the colours were shimmering and so very vibrant. I felt such incredible joy from him. He wanted me to understand his experience. I felt his happiness. I couldn't ignore it. It was like he picked up the phone to tell me, like he was at school and he was learning the most amazing things. He wanted to involve me. That's what it felt like.

He also wanted to give some direction about his Celebration of Life, which we'd planned for the following Saturday.

> *"Mum, if you're going to talk the talk, you had better be ready to walk the walk."*

We had planned to hold the Celebration in a large local church. Jamie communicated that he wanted each family member to sit at the front of the church on chairs facing the congregation. He asked that we each choose a song to play before we spoke to the gathering. We all chose a song. I chose "I Hope You Dance" by Lee Ann Womack. It seemed fitting because I truly hoped he was dancing somewhere. And then we were to speak our words. Jamie was very directive and he made it clear to me he wanted to be involved in the planning of his service.

On May 25, the anniversary of my father's death, we sat at the front of the church and spoke our words just as Jamie had asked. There were over six hundred people present, all looking at our little family group. Jamie had touched so many people in his short life. Taylor May was front and centre in the congregation with Lindsay's mum. I looked back at all the faces.

It was very comforting to have so many people come to honour Jamie. There were people who got up to speak. We heard many stories about Jamie that we would have never heard if it hadn't been for the courage of these individuals. He was so loved. One story in particular touched my heart. Jamie loved clothes and bought a lot of it. When he was finished with some clothing, he would contact a local counsellor who'd pass them on to young men being released from prison in Vancouver.

She said he wanted the men to feel good about themselves when they re-entered the world. He never told us he was doing this. That was the kind of man he was.

The minister finally had to encourage people to sit down. So many still wanted to speak, but the service needed to come to an end. There was a gathering after the ceremony. In the church, there were tables of food provided by the nurses at the hospital, along with many others who worked there. I was so overwhelmed with the outpouring of love we received from our community. It made me realize why it's so important to have rituals involving death and bereavement. I would never have heard the stories told by so many people. Those stories would have been lost forever.

One person approached me after the service, and she said, "I never thought I would feel better after a funeral than I did before going in. But I feel like I know your son so much better now." It was a beautiful thing to say to me in that moment.

Funeral rituals were studied by the team of Charles Corr, Charles Nabe and Donna Corr,[4] and they developed tasks associated with funeral rituals. The task that was helpful to me was "making real the implications of death." I was struggling with acceptance and the Celebration made it much more real to me. I couldn't have known how much it would help until I lived through it. The gathering of family and friends, the stories told, the eulogies we gave as a family created a place to land after a week of chaos. I am so glad we took the time and found the strength to make it happen.

When we got home, we saw someone had called while we were gone. The number read 111-111-1111. I couldn't imagine who would be calling because everyone we knew had been at the Celebration. I called the operator

---

[4] Charles A. Corr, Clyde M. Nabe and Donna M. Corr, "A task-based approach for understanding and evaluating funeral practices," *Thanatos* 19, no. 2 (1994): 10–15.

and she said there was no such number sequence but if it registered on our phone it had to have originated somewhere. I called Lindsay and she said 1111 was Jamie's pager number. I was stunned. Since then I've noticed the clock when it says 1:11 or 11:11. In doing some research, I found this type of number sequence is one way those on the other side communicate. I believe on his day of celebration, Jamie wanted us to know he was with us.

Within a short time, late one night, another message came from Jamie. I wrote it down in my journal.

May 30, 2002

The challenge is in the balance. When you are too close to the bottom, all you can see is the bottom. It's a thin line to walk, but it will soon become clear, much like murky water—when the dirt settles to the bottom, the top water is clear. I think our communication doesn't need to be questioned, as you are questioning now. It will come in different forms. Pay attention—some of it is very subtle. Encourage each other to talk. Remember to ask for help because it's limitless from where I stand.

I understand your humanness. But there can be so much pain on that level. That's why it was so difficult to walk on that plane. Keep up the good work. I know it's not easy. Remember the balance; the meditation will help and so will music. I love you all so much. I am as close as breathing. Shut your eyes and I am there. Mum, don't doubt yourself. It is this easy.

It was as if Jamie put his arms around me and whispered in my ear, *"It's all good, Mum"*—as if I was an out-of-control horse running towards a very ugly place, and he threw a lasso around me and reeled me in.

Having a child and watching him develop and grow to be an adult doesn't come without the risk of losing him—or does it? Do we just assume we will be spared? When it happens to someone else, it's a sad story. When it happens to you, it's beyond comprehension. It's like your head understands the reality, but your heart looks for alternatives. My heart ached for the child I gave birth to. It was not such a sharp pain anymore as it had been in the first few days. It was more like a steady ache. The tears were never far, but more controlled.

Five days before he died, he came to see me on Mother's Day. He ate a whole can of smoked oysters! To this day, I can't eat oysters. He lay Taylor on the floor and played with her. She laughed and looked at him with loving eyes. I didn't know this was the last time I would see my son.

Another communication came in:

> Oh Mum, I think you've got it, then you start drifting backwards. It's no less true now than it was when I contacted you for the first time. I'm okay—actually more than okay. It's peaceful here for me. Don't be sad; my struggle is over, but yours continues. It doesn't have to be sad and heavy. The choice is yours. You just can't see me, but you can hear what I'm saying. Get out of the sun now; you're burning!

This made me laugh, as indeed, I had been writing in the sun and my skin was beginning to turn red.

Acceptance. I think that is truly the secret when something like a death happens. If you try and fight it, it won't work and you will stay in a personal hell for as long as you try. I couldn't bring Jamie back. I couldn't change what had happened. I couldn't fix it.

I was gentle with myself and it helped to keep me out of the terror. The secret was in staying calm and not being caught up in the chaos of my mind.

The truth was still harsh. It was unbelievable that it had just been over three weeks since Jamie was killed.

June 12, 2002

> Mum, you know the truth. You've always known my truth. Now it's just clearer. It's how it was meant to be. I am free now. I love you and I love my family. That was so good. But this is the form I need to take now. My journey on earth ended at the most perfect moment. My moment. Just like 12:34, February 5, 1973, was my perfect moment to enter the world. You, my family, are all doing so well. I feel such pride. Keep together. I know you all love me and your love will be forever more. Don't

look for things to make you sad. I watch you and sometimes you feel you need to be sad. Be joyful—be happy.

I thought about the morning of May 18, before I knew he was dead, when I had gone to get dressed and bumped into his spirit in my bedroom. "No, no, no," I said. *It can't be.*

But it was.

June 15, 2002

So do you see the big picture yet? When you watch the waves on the lake does it begin to make sense? We are part of such a bigger whole. We play a part, but we are not the picture. Each of us is as important as the next because together we form the big picture.

The threads of our lives are woven into a tapestry that has been alive since the beginning of time. We sense we are individual, but we're not really because if one thread is broken, the tapestry would begin to unweave. When we die, we do not break the thread. We just don't walk on your plane. But that's what I mean by the big picture. You are focused only on earth, but the unseen and the unknown form just as an important role. If earth was the only dimension, what would be the point? Do you see, really see? Look beyond what you know to be true and you will see me. I'm still in the picture, just not on earth.

Mum, I know you are beginning to find peace in all of this. Just relax and stop worrying about the details.

Dad, keep believing, keep searching. You are on the right path. Just like Mum thought this afternoon on the beach. You were a good father and continue to be.

Sean and Lisa, rise up above the clutter. Focus on your own lives. You are building together and will find your own answers.

Lindsay, this is the work I talked about. Don't give up when it gets hard. It will all be worth it in the end. You will become a new person with strength beyond your wildest dreams. Your family won't even recognize you, but I will. And sweet Taylor, you already know.

Keep trying, Mum.

I started to cry.

"Don't do that, Mum," he said. *"It will make you too heavy to lift you to where I am."*

"I miss you. I'm sorry, Jamie. I'm human."

I felt so heavy and, like blowing out a candle, he was gone.

I realized what he was saying to me. I had to raise my vibration high enough to reach him, and he had to lower his frequency to meet me where I was. Joy and happiness are the highest frequencies, and grief, sadness and fear are at the bottom of the scale. But I had to be gentle with myself. I wanted to feel him, but I also knew I had to grieve and feel the sadness. I was finding acceptance in many ways, but there was one particular thing that I struggled so hard with.

When Jamie died, it wasn't possible for me to see his body. He died in the fire of the accident. When I was at the funeral home, I said I really needed to touch him. They said I couldn't do this. I didn't want to think about why I was denied my request. It was so painful to visualize what remained of his body. But I wanted so badly to touch him. I ached to hug him one more time. A short time after, Jamie came to me in a dream. I walked over to him and put my arms around him. He did the same and he felt solid, like he did when he was alive. It felt so good to be able to do that. He made it possible for me to hug him one more time. I found so much peace in that. Jamie found many ways to visit me when I least expected it.

In the past, I've shared this dream with other people who've experienced loss. For those who have not had a dream experience with their loved one, some are concerned about the lack of this connection. Researchers Joshua Black, Kathryn Belicki and Jessica Emberley-Ralph[5] looked at grief and dream recall. They identified people's concerns that "they haven't crossed over

---

[5] Joshua Black, Kathryn Belicki and Jessica Emberley-Ralph, "Who dreams of the deceased? The roles of dream recall, grief intensity, attachment, and openness to experience," *Dreaming* 29, no. 1 (March 2019): 57–78, https://psycnet.apa.org/record/2019-14239-004.

yet" and "perhaps they don't love me." The researchers found that those who dreamed of the deceased tended to dream more frequently anyway. They also determined that those who were open to unconventional events also had an increase in these type of dreams. Most of these people indicated the dreams tended to be very positive in nature. I found it interesting that those with a high insecure anxious attachment style (the attachment style that fits me best) had a better chance of experiencing post-death dreams.

On July 2, 2002, I wrote in my journal that I couldn't believe how long it had been since I'd written—two weeks. I wondered if that meant that life was better. I knew we were receiving gifts on a daily basis from all that had happened. The rawness was not as painful. It's like there was depth to the experience. I wanted to feel joy for myself and for Jamie. I did believe he wanted us to be happy. I could only guess that was what I would want for him if the roles were reversed.

July 4, 2002

Jamie came today and sang "Happy Birthday" to me. I cried. He said, "Enough of that. " He said he wanted to give a piece of what he felt. Instantly energy surged through every cell of my body. I felt waves of ecstasy like nothing I had ever felt before. He said I was to receive a gift and that I was ready to do so. It was wonderful! I felt so blessed.

July 14, 2002

We had no unfinished business, you and I. We were always up to date with our relationship. You were so right—"I was not ordinary"—and from where I am now, I know you aren't either. You still have so much to accomplish before you join me. So many lives to touch. I am happy. My work was finished, and didn't I pack a lot into twenty-nine years! I lived more than many live in a lifetime. Grandma will join me soon. She's ready. She knows she's never going "to get it" and she is okay to come. She wasn't supposed to get it. She will leave quickly and will not suffer. She will just go to sleep. Be prepared, Mum. It will be hard on you because you will still be processing my passing. It is so easy to talk to you. You are so open to receive. I don't need to shout my message.

Sometimes I felt myself getting stronger and then I would fall backwards again. But I kept getting up and dusting myself off.

I was so glad I didn't have regrets about what I did and didn't say to Jamie. He was right. We were up to date with our relationship. We didn't always agree on everything, but we could always talk. It is so important to have conversations with those we love, as hard as it might be. Once a person dies, there's no opportunity to speak with them in human form. We never know when the day will be the last day. It might be as simple as telling a person you love them or it might be words of forgiveness. It doesn't really matter what it is. Authentic dialogue may take courage, but words unsaid will never be heard. So, if you have something to say to someone, say it now.

July 15, 2002

Don't you see the remarkable work you can do on your plane? Few are awake enough to understand what this is about. You have a strength beyond most. You have been waiting all your life.

We had this work to do and we agreed. Don't you see, Mum? The body is just a vehicle for the work. I did what I had to do when I was on earth. Now we are like a tag team. You still have a body and I will help.

I see you cry and I do understand. But we are just like dance partners at our own celebration. It's all good, Mum. I'm right here helping you do what needs to be done. You know this and it's as if I am right beside you. It's the work, Mum. We played the game according to the planet's rules. I was your son; you were my mother. Now we have a greater understanding. We think we are born as families and we are, but the greater work is done in partnership with the other side. There is a greater purpose to all of this. We get so caught up in the obvious. But that's not the point. If it was, it would be so trivial. What is this all about? It's a partnership with the unknown, with the side you can't see. That's all. We are mother and son, but we are so much more than that. We agreed to be partners many many worlds ago. And now do you see? You had to love me as much as you did so you could break through by feeling so much pain. Mum, I'm not gone. I am as close as your breathing. We are mother and son because it fits as the world sees fit. They understand loss and grief and pain. But that is not our lesson. It's not yours. It's just an agreement. Sean understands. He recognized me right from the beginning. He knew me because he knew me long before he was born. He is so wise, so loving. And Mum, we are all part of the whole. Sean knows on some level. Remind him, Mum. He will walk the earth for many many years because he has so much to offer the people on earth. We always recognized each other; right from the beginning he knew me. We have been together for decades, eons, lifetimes.

Tell him how much I love him. But you know, he feels it through his heart. And his Lisa, she is an incredible woman. She is the only person on earth who can truly appreciate Sean. She has a special insight. She is the only one for him. Don't let life get in the way of your truth because you knew right from the beginning of your life. You knew truth. Mum, you can hardly hold on to your pen because this is coming so fast.

I guess I was beginning to understand the part that pain plays. Was I strong? You bet, in the truest sense of the word. Hit me again, world! I would just keep bouncing back because it was the only way. I never knew how strong I was until I was put to the test.

On July 18, 2002, I wrote in my journal. I talked about the fact that it had been two months since Jamie walked on earth and yet is seemed like a lifetime. It was so unreal. It felt like it had been years. So much life had been lived in such a short time. I thought, *Was it only a summer since he left?* I felt like he still might come running in the door. He would say, "Mum, I haven't got much time." I can still see him pushing the carriage down the street on the last Mother's Day, less than a week before he left. He had Taylor in the buggy, his dog on a leash and a diaper bag slung over his shoulder. He was happy.

A change in perception can make such a difference in how you view things. I was given an opportunity to find out just how powerful this can be.

In 2000, I had decided to buy a new car. I decided to give the old white Honda to Jamie. It was the car he was driving when he was killed. In the months that followed, I seemed to see white 1990 Honda vehicles on a regular basis. Each time one passed, I felt such sadness. About six months later, I was sitting in the hairdressers and a white Honda went past.

A small voice inside said, *"Instead of feeling sad, consider that I might just be saying hello whenever you see my car."*

It was such a small shift in perception, but it created a new experience for me. Every time I saw one, I would smile and feel Jamie's presence. White 1990 Hondas are still on the road. It says a great deal about the Honda manufacturers, but it also says a great deal about the fact that life goes on whether you're grieving or not.

The summer of 2002, I spent time at the lake. When I was in the water I could hear Jamie saying, *"You are a part of nature when you're in the lake. I told you this was a healing place."* And indeed, the water brought a great comfort to me. At times, I would go into the nearby forest and hug the trees. I could feel their pulse and it felt so good. It made me realize how far I had come in such a short time.

I put one foot in front of the other, literally. I had been walking for years, always the same route. Ironically Jamie bought a house on one of the streets that was on my walking route. As the years went by, I saw things change in the house. At first, he lived there with a friend and I would see cars and jeeps parked outside. Then he and Lindsay lived in the house and brought Taylor home from the hospital. Sometimes I would stop by and visit with them during my walk. After Jamie's death, it was hard to go by the house, but I knew Taylor and Lindsay were inside and that made things easier.

Soon Taylor learned to stand. I would see her waving in the window. I still walk past the house eighteen years later.

Jamie was an amazing man. He packed a great deal into his short twenty-nine years. I once had an astrology reading done for him a few months before he died. The reader said his life path showed he was interested in so many things. She described his life like a smorgasbord and he was tasting every-thing he could get his hands on. I laughed about that at the time because it described him well. From where I stand now, I understand sometimes it's only after an event that we realize the subtle prompts along the way. According to his astrological chart, Jamie lived life fully. I wonder if it showed he wouldn't be here to see his thirtieth birthday.

August 4, 2002

To be present with your loneliness is painful but necessary. You will learn nothing by avoiding it. It won't make you stronger. I know it's hard. Just like Sean said in the beginning, "There is nowhere to hide." It will get better. This summer is your time to heal, so you can do the work. If you run from the painful feelings, it will just take longer. You are human and must experience the pain. I am not—but I do know your pain. There was no other way for me to leave. You know that and so do I. The difference is that you feel my loss. I don't feel yours. I know that is hard for you to understand. But I am closer to you now than I could ever have been on earth. I surround you and my feelings for you are beyond words. So I don't miss you because you are right here with me. Remember it works both ways. I am also right with you. Sometimes you don't feel me close because I am doing my work. But when you do need me, I can be as close as breathing—what you are feeling right now. So stay at the lake, be with your feelings, be with yourself.

When you came down to the beach a couple of hours ago, there were people and children all around you. Now the sun has gone down and you are the only one left. But look at the lake, Mum. It's still there right in front of you. It never left, and like the lake, neither did I.

The next morning there was a coolness in the air. I wondered if my healing would have been harder and longer without the lake. I thought it probably would have been. And so I called this my summer of healing and of growth and of understanding. The lake helped to heal me. Nature is truly a remarkable gift.

Three months had passed. It seemed like three years. It had been so long since I'd seen Jamie. I knew it was important not to dwell too much on that. The trailer at the lake was so important that summer. So perfect, so close to nature. It had been such a good place to be. I could feel the fall coming on.

One day I saw a man sitting at a nearby picnic table. I squinted my eyes and thought it could have been Jamie. Muscle shirt, ball cap, beautiful smile. It wasn't Jamie. I saw a fellow on a motorcycle. It looked like it might be Jamie. Another time, driving in the university, a man with his head down was gardening. He looked just like Jamie. I stopped and opened my window to call to him and then realized it couldn't possibly be him. John Bowlby[6] calls this phenomenon "separation distress." It involves a strong urge to search for the deceased person. A face can just "pop" out of the crowd as you hope to re-establish physical closeness to them. It provides temporary relief from the sorrow of the loss. It may happen for a few months after the death until the reality has enough time to permeate your mind more fully. It's a natural response, but it can take you off guard.

Since that time, I've learned this is not unusual. It happens to many people when they're trying to process their grief. It's part of the searching and yearning.

August 21, 2002

That's right, Mum. It's important that you remember I have the best, especially when you start feeling sad. I am peaceful, happy. It's beyond anything you can imagine. Keep working; you will get through this, one day at a time. The hardest part is behind you. I'm not saying what you're experiencing right now is easy, but it's better and will continue to get better. Have faith. I'm so glad you spend time at the lake. It's so good for you.

I learned grief was not a linear process. One day I felt gratitude and could focus on living and the next day I felt such overwhelming pain and found

---

[6] John Bowlby, *Attachment and loss: sadness and depression, volume 3* (New York: Basic Books, 1980).

myself lost. It was unpredictable. I never knew what the day would bring when I got up in the morning.

This situation is described by Margaret Stroebe and Henk Schut.[7] Their research shows these behaviours fall into a dual process model—two main ways of coping that a person switches between. There's an oscillation, or swinging, between coping mechanisms that are loss-oriented and restoration-oriented. In a loss-oriented coping mechanism, you think about the loss and feel the grief and may avoid everyday activities. A restoration-oriented coping mechanism would be thinking or doing something other than focusing on your grief: attending to life tasks, learning new things and creating new roles. As you oscillate between the two, it helps you deal with the grief bit by bit.

It can help to know what's happening. It helps with the out-of-control feeling that often occurs.

September 18, 2002

It is four months today. It's amazing how time has gone by. Or perhaps has not gone by. The highs and lows are incredible. Today my brother, Pete, gave us the cremation box for Jamie's ashes. It's so beautiful. Pete spent his whole life working with wood. The box was dark wood. He had sanded and lacquered the outside. It was put together with such care. It must have taken him many hours to craft such a piece. He made it for us. I love him for doing that.

I picked up Jamie's ashes at the funeral home. I bought a silver heart and they put some of his ashes in it. I had taken Pete's beautiful box to the funeral home earlier. It made it much easier to take Jamie home with me. When I picked it up, it was so heavy I cried. It reminded me of how heavy we are on earth. I guess since his death, I had thought of him as so light. And he is now.

---

[7] Margaret Stroebe and Henk Schut, "The dual process model of coping with bereavement: rationale and description," *Death Studies* 23, no. 3 (April–May 1999): 197–224, https://pubmed.ncbi.nlm.nih.gov/10848151/.

November 2, 2002

I'm cozy all the time. I can't come to your level in human form, but you can come to mine by being light. You feel sad tonight because you want me with you. But I am with you and I always will be. You saw what you wanted to see. I came to earth to teach. When my teaching was complete, it was time for me to go. I couldn't have felt more loved. I knew that I was an important part of your family. But my purpose was fulfilled and I am home now. Please forgive me for the pain. I didn't mean to hurt you, but it had to be this way. I am happy. I am at peace. I wish I could help you more. I know your pain, but thank you for allowing me to be part of you. It made the journey so much easier on earth. I am free now and it feels so good. I am home and someday you will be too.

By December, Taylor May was crawling and pulling herself up to stand. She laughed out loud. Her weight was twenty-two pounds. She loved squash and green beans and *Teletubbies* on TV. She had a smile that lit up the whole world.

December 2002

Taylor came over today. She ate mashed potatoes and mashed carrots sitting in Sean and Jamie's old childhood highchair. It all seemed so right. Jamie was with us as if he was in human form. He didn't miss a thing. I'm so glad I have that. It's just a thin veil. Thank you, Jamie Ross.

That Christmas I couldn't bring myself to put up a Christmas tree. I couldn't open our Christmas box and look at the ornaments from years gone by. I knew one that would especially bring me to tears. It was a baby jar that Jamie had made into a Santa at preschool when he was five years old. There was a Santa head glued on the top and the jar became the body. Jamie had been so proud of his creation. He burst in the door from school and proudly showed me his masterpiece. Sean was especially pleased because in the jar there were glorious little white and red peppermint candies. Jamie always shared whatever he had with his little brother. They were a team.

So I didn't bring out the little Santa with the black felt belt. I didn't put up any lights. But I did light candles in memory of the work we had all done in the past seven months and to honour our son.

Alan D. Wolfelt[8] writes about healing holiday grief. Don't judge yourself or set your expectations too high. Let your grief be what it is and let yourself—your new grieving self—be who you are. Powerful advice.

December 24, 2002

Mum, keep going. Keep on track. Yesterday I was with you holding sparklers and I wanted you to know how much I love you and that I am so proud of you. It's hard work and I know this. Meditate more, Mum, and you can see for yourself. It's all so simple, what really counts. Love, that's all. And I knew and continue to know love. I had and have it all. And so do you. Merry Christmas, Mum.

I felt so incredibly lucky that I could hear what Jamie was telling me. He was encouraging and supportive just when I needed to hear his words. He seemed to know.

And so our first Christmas without Jamie was over. We knew Jamie didn't want us to be sad. Sean and Lisa put on a beautiful Christmas dinner. We went up Christmas morning and Greg helped Sean stuff the turkey. It was a beautiful day. There was such a good feeling in the house. Lindsay phoned to tell us she woke up this morning with Taylor sitting up and saying, "Hi Dad," and she was waving. Lindsay also said she heard Taylor laughing and then she heard Jamie's laugh.

December 30, 2002

It's time to step up to the plate. To open your mind, to look at what your work is. The veil will become extremely thin and you will "see" what needs to be done. Your resting time is over. You have become extremely strong due to your challenges. Your eyes, heart and soul are open. You are ready to work with me. Get ready, set, go!

---

[8] Alan D. Wolfelt, *Healing your holiday grief: 100 practical ideas for blending mourning and celebration during the holiday season* (Fort Collins: Companion Press, 2005).

January 4, 2003

Lindsay told us she is moving back to Red Deer. I cried and then decided I had to support her choice. Taylor came today and I babysat. I'm trying to understand. I realize Lindsay needs to be close to her own family. It's such a difficult time for her. She's a new mother. She has had such loss. She is trying to be brave, but it can't be easy for her. Taylor! She is such a bright light in our lives. We will miss them both so much. But maybe it can't be about us.

I want to start my master's degree. I guess now is as good as any time. I need to focus on my life. I want to focus on death and dying. I can see how things have fallen into place. My interest now makes more sense than ever. I want to help others deal with this thing called death.

I decided I would apply to start my Master of Science in Nursing the next year. It was time to step forward and continue living my life. The next stage was about to unfold.

I wanted to grow from the ashes of my life. There had been enough pain. I wanted to stop hurting so much and find some joy. I knew Jamie wanted that too.

The next day, a student stayed after class. She hesitantly approached me.

"I need to tell you something," she said. "I know it might seem strange, but you have to know what I saw today. When you were up at the front of the class, I saw a misty figure in the corner of the room. At one point, he came over and surrounded you with a hug. I have always been able to see those on the other side. I had to tell you."

I found great comfort in her words.

"Thank you for having the courage to share your message," I said.

And so the day came that would have been Jamie's thirtieth birthday. I wondered how that would have been on this side. He never seemed to be too concerned about age, so maybe turning thirty wouldn't have bothered him.

On the other side, it felt like he had been happy for a long time. I sensed his joy, his playful attitude. He was light, freer than he had ever been and able to do all. He did the things he always wanted to do. The things he valued the most like compassion and love were part of him, what he had become.

February 5, 2003

The more you open up, the greater the access to others on this side. There is such great knowledge to share and it's everyone's knowledge. We are truly of one breath—on earth and on this side.

So don't be sad on my birthday. It was only a day to change form. I am happy. I am with you every day. Taylor is the only one who can see me. But Mum, I was very close on May 18 in your bedroom. You sensed me so close because I still had some denseness. I am so light now that I am subtle when I am close. But I am here, as close as breathing. Know this to be true. I feel like I need to be very clear, especially today. I am close and will help you live this day. It's of no importance to me. It means nothing now, just a date. But I understand it's not as easy for you on earth. Let it go, enjoy each other, think of me, but please don't be sad. It's so different here. I am always at peace, always warm, always cozy like I never knew on earth. It's all just remembered when you cross over. It's what has always been. Earth is the school. Know this to be true.

Celebrate my existence. Do not grieve my passing over.

I smiled when I received these words. Jamie always had a wisdom that preceded his chronological age. He felt so deeply and completely while he was with us in human form. I could see how his thinking was leaking between the two dimensions called heaven and earth. Was this his work on the other side? He always seemed so clear when he wanted to get a message across to me. I didn't tell too many people about what happened because I thought they would think I was crazy. Perhaps they might think it was my grief talking, not my son. But I knew how this came through and I couldn't ignore it. I couldn't brush it off because it would seem like such a wasteful thing to do with the gift he was giving. Maybe one day I would share this with other people. But right now it was too personal. I didn't want to break the spell. If I shared it now, it might disappear. He might disappear.

February 12, 2003

Darling Taylor turned one today. Happy Birthday, Taylor. Lindsay brought the baby over today for a visit. Sean came and you could see her love for him. It was so neat to watch them together. I guess it was a little like it might have been with Jamie. It healed us all, maybe even Jamie. She knew us and was so comfortable. I wished it could last forever. But I knew nothing lasts forever. Nothing! I treasured each moment I had with her.

When I think back, I wonder if my pain was so great, so overwhelming, that I didn't see my husband's pain, his grief. It was as if all I could do was to live my own path and let him find his way by himself. I think he was doing the same thing. He was just surviving.

February 13, 2003

Tonight Greg came into the kitchen and asked me what I thought Jamie would be wearing if I could see him. I said I thought he might be wearing a robe. Greg said his heart began to race because a few moments earlier, someone had stood behind him in a purple robe, broad shoulders, hood covering the face. I knew it was Jamie. Some things you just know to be true. I am not sure if your senses are profoundly awakened when you live through a tragic event, but I do know my attention was more focused on the unseen. At the same time, I still struggled with my humanness. I wanted him to come home and yet, on some elusive level, I knew he was "home." I felt like that is what Jamie was trying to tell me. If I could just release him with joy, I could really begin the work.

In the past, I received messages from the other side, but I didn't always know who they were from. The messages just came. When I asked a question, the answer often came. Here was the answer I heard that day. It wasn't Jamie. I'm not sure who it was. It was warm and loving and it said:

> *You need to fully love and accept yourself just as you are. You need to think green thoughts, picture a wonderful scene in the forest. Be aware of all the shades of green—see the sun filtering through the trees. Smell the earth rich with its gifts. See the path. The one that leads you on your journey.*

> *It's safe. Don't be afraid. It's a path you have travelled before. You've just forgotten the details. The messages are unspoken. Jamie is a part of all this. He is not your personal messenger, but he is part of the message. We have welcomed him back. He plays such an important part in this next step. So in a breath, you are carried forward. It's just beginning. Watch for the signs.*

Taylor stayed the weekend. She slept with me each night. Once during the night, I woke up and she was sitting up in bed, laughing and waving. I felt Jamie in the room. She looked past me, waved, and said, "Hi Dad." She was only thirteen months old. It was comforting to watch her communicate with her father. I have learned you can't hold on to anything but love. And Jamie's love for his daughter was so real. I watched Taylor feel it. She could sense him in our bedroom. How could someone so young recognize her father? It must have been because she didn't have the filters that we develop as we grow older. I like to think she just understood it was her father's energy she felt. How wonderful was that!

I decided that my journal could be a two-way street. If Jamie could come through in the writing, then I should be able to reach him the same way.

March 2003

> Jamie, I think that you can communicate through my journal just like I listen to you. You were and continue to be an important part of my life. I'm beginning to understand what this is all about. I guess it had to be this way. But you were such an incredible part of my life. You taught me; I taught you. You taught me about fun, about living on the edge. You brought me out of my comfort zone. And

that you did, and that you continue to do, even from the other side.

Jamie, how come I'm still here and you're not? Will Sean bury us all? I always thought you'd be there to support him and he could support you. I feel sad that he doesn't have you—on earth, I mean. I know he has you in another form. He knows it too.

I guess I always thought my love would be strong enough to protect you. Protect you from pain, from the negative side of life. I couldn't have loved you more.

I spend so much of my life trying to deal with the truth of the situation. There's not a day that goes by that I don't think about you. It's so different from losing my dad. I loved him, but not like I loved you. He was my father; you are my child.

You have reconnected with your purpose. Thank you for touching my life. It might not have happened that way. It truly is a gift, isn't it, Jamie? It might never have been. You stopped here for a short time so I could be your mother. Thank you for allowing that to be. It makes the years so much more precious. I was chosen. I can see that now. Thank you. It took a lot for you to stop with us. I can see that now.

You were never meant to live to be an old man. On some level, it's beginning to make sense. Thank you for choosing us to be your family.

It's almost more than I can comprehend. But on so many levels, I understand. It's just hard because I'm so connected to earth. But I know this to be the truth. Jamie, I release you back to where you came. I can't believe how much better I feel. This letter to you seemed to release something.

I had surrendered.

October 27, 2003

I drove out to Chase; I wanted to stop at the accident scene one more time. Every time I went to do this, Jamie would whisper in my ear, *"It's not good for you, Mum. Don't stop. I am not there."* But the urge was so strong. I wanted to stop just one more time. As I drove along the highway, I caught sight of a white pickup truck in my rear-view mirror. It was the type of truck Jamie had once owned. The truck was so close to my rear bumper. I couldn't make out the face of the person who was driving. The scene of the accident was on a straight stretch of the road. I thought, *If this truck doesn't stop following so close, I'm not going to be able to stop when I want to.* Just then I went right past the spot where I wanted to stop. I looked again in my rear view and the white truck had vanished into thin air. There were no crossroads where it could have turned off. Nothing but fields on both sides of the road. I thought, *Where did that truck go? It was right behind me.* Then I heard a voice that was familiar. *"Mum, I told you it wasn't good for you to stop."* Wow! I guess I had better start listening more carefully.

To this day, I have never stopped at that spot again ... On December 13, 2003, we found out Greg had bowel cancer, stage 3.

December 13, 2003

I will not leave you. You only need to ask. I am here. Know you are home; it's safe. Always come back to me if you're not feeling strong. And so, Mum, it will be okay even if it doesn't feel like that right now. Be strong. Keep going. I am right here beside you. You can't control this. Just live your life. The rest will fall into place. We love you and we love Dad too.

Hepatic flexure adenocarcinoma, stage 3—all the words, so many words. What did it mean? It meant Greg had a thirty percent chance of surviving, even with surgery and chemotherapy. It was such a harsh reality. After hearing the diagnosis, the first thing Greg said was *'I guess I had better get my Christmas* shopping done." It was such a brave response. I was so frightened, I could hardly breathe.

How was this my life? I hardly recognized myself, such a huge amount of sadness. I wondered where all of this was going. I knew I had to be very careful to protect myself. It was all so new. I felt like my world was falling apart again. I couldn't believe I could lose Greg.

I was trying to understand why I needed to live through this. I had worked so hard at accepting Jamie's death. Now I had to walk this path with Greg. How could I help myself through this process? We had so much history. It was hard to know where I started and he left off. We would get through this, just like we had with everything else in our lives.

On December 20, Greg had two feet of bowel removed, along with four lymph nodes. When we went to see him in the hospital, he looked so pale, so sick. Sean and Lisa brought him a huge picture of Taylor to put on the wall. He started to laugh but had to put a quick stop to that because his stitches started to pull. Taylor could always make him smile.

Greg was discharged from the hospital on December 24. I cooked a turkey and Sean and Lisa came for dinner. All Greg could handle was cream of mushroom soup. But he was so happy to be home again with his family.

On February 5, 2004, it was Jamie's birthday. It was funny—it didn't hurt. I almost felt guilty but I wondered if that was exactly what I was supposed to feel. I felt him on a very different level.

What a time this had been. So many lessons, so many tests. Most of the time I felt pretty lucky. I felt like I was winning this battle with life. And that was exactly what it felt like, a battle. I knew it was all exactly as it needed to be. I knew I must be aware of the blessings I had in my life. It was just that it was so intense, or maybe it had always been intense. It seemed like the past two years had brought such sadness. It hadn't been spread over a lifetime. It had been compacted. But maybe that was the only way it would have worked—the lessons, the blessings. I just needed to trust and that's all.

February 12, 2004

Mum, it will be okay. Don't worry so much. This has been written already. Dad contracted for this so many lives ago. He's better with it than you are. You need to remember that. Let go of all that concern. In his heart of hearts, he knows this is the way it has to go. Don't worry. You'll make yourself sick without having to. I am with you both. Let go and let Spirit guide you. It's all right.

On February 15, 2004, Greg started his chemo treatment. He had chosen to start a clinical drug trial. The chemotherapy drugs were only given to those in the trial. Greg felt if he could help others by doing this, it would all be worthwhile. Even with the drugs, the doctor said he only had a thirty percent chance of survival. We were hopeful. It had been quite a journey. So long since a Wednesday had just been a Wednesday. I decreased my work to part time so I could go with Greg for his treatments. I also took a leave from my master's studies. I couldn't do it all. I needed to look after myself so I could look after him.

May 18, 2004, I sat in the backyard with the beautiful pine trees. It was a spectacular morning, much like the one two years before. I closed my eyes and could hear Jamie say, *"Mum, keep going. Remember the good. It's all good."*

I remembered all I had, not what I didn't have. The connection with Jamie was still strong. I didn't want to feel sad, but I wanted to honour my son and his life.

Maybe that's the secret to understanding. If he was here so I could put my arms around him, he would also be part of the struggle on this plane. He walked the earth for twenty-nine years. We got to love him and know him. Then his time was up and he left. But before he went, he brought his beautiful daughter into the world as a parting gift, a piece of himself to share with us. She was a generous offering to help us through a most difficult time so we could see some light in our darkest times, so we didn't all lose our way, to make the unbearable a little more bearable.

On August 13, I watched the sun come up. There was a gentle breeze. The pages of my life unfolded. It was interesting to me that some people received this day and others didn't. Some had yesterday, but some won't have today.

Death. Everyone seems to voice such fear, but is it because we don't know? If we did, would people be leaving in great numbers, catching the next express train to heaven? Jamie's main message was about his joy, his peace and the love he felt all around him. Do we just forget about all of that when we enter the world? Maybe that's why we aren't given the information. Maybe that's why young children stop talking about heaven at age two. They would give away the "big secret" if they didn't stop remembering and telling us about it. Was Taylor beginning to forget?

Today was the last visit to Kelowna for Greg's chemo. I felt Jamie was in the car driving home. He was bouncing up and down, so excited.

"Remember, Mum," he said, *"I share the joy, too."*

It made me cry to feel him so close. He was indeed sharing our joy—Greg's treatment was over. It was such a relief. We didn't know what the future would bring, but we did know he was still alive and were so grateful for that. I started back to work teaching full time and resumed my master's studies.

May 18, 2005

Don't hold on to your sadness, Mum. It never ends—you and me. Don't be sad. I am closer now than ever. It's all in how you look at it. Three months, three years, three minutes, there is no time. Just air, space and each other. The connection cannot be broken. Believe what you are hearing. In a blink of an eye and you'll see what I see. The beauty of what is, the reality of truth and light. No pain, no sorrow, only wholeness, contentment, love and peace like no other.

Believe in me as I believe in you. We just walk in different realities for now, but that will change—when it's right. Open yourself up to receive—you'll see—beyond your wildest dreams, beyond your expectations. Let go and know I am here—no different than May 18, 2002, just a breath away.

These words helped. It must seem so simple to him where he is. When all the games, fears and expectations drop by the wayside, only truth remains. That's what I felt from him. I felt so lucky to be able to receive Jamie's teachings.

"Believe in me as I believe in you."

I thought about that for a while. I needed to have faith in this process.

That was the last detailed transmission I had from Jamie. He had been giving the same message for the past two years. He was happy and felt at home where he was. To this day, I still receive short brief messages. Sometimes it's in the form of a symbol or a few words.

Spontaneous communication began when I was a young woman and Bert, my next door neighbour, made himself known to me. Over the years, there have been others, so when this happened with Jamie it didn't scare me.

June 5, 2005

I had an amazing dream last night. I was sitting downstairs on the couch. The door from the garage opened and someone walked down the hall. It's Jamie! He walked into the playroom, turned and faced me. It was his beautiful face. I was stunned. I said, "Oh my God, it's really you!" I put my hand over my mouth. He said nothing, but messages were silently passed. I couldn't repeat the messages out loud. There were no words on this plane. I was beginning to understand that some things are beyond the words we know on earth. The thought patterns seem to be what was transferred back and forth.

I could sense another chapter of my life was opening up. And it was happening because I had found a "new normal." This new way of being had created a new identity for me. Jamie's leaving had transformed me in so many ways. I was less anxious. I was living through my worst nightmare and I knew that nothing could ever be as damaging to me as what I had experienced in the past few years. I could survive anything. I never knew this before. I had not been challenged to dig so deep before in my life. I was digging deep and finding great treasure buried deep inside myself. There was a strength I never knew existed. I was able to see how things could have been worse. I found profound gratitude for what I did have in my life. Things I took for granted were now deeply appreciated. I found deep compassion for myself as I bounced back and forth between appreciation and despair.

I thought I needed to remember as much about him as I could so I could tell Taylor what kind of man her father was. I pictured telling her when she was older.

I would say, "He loved you so much, Taylor. Every time I went to the house, he always had you in his arms. It was as if he didn't want to let you go. He slept with you on his chest. He gave you baths. He gave you bottles. It made my heart so happy to see him as your father. To be a father was something he talked about all his life, even when he was just a little boy. I think there was a magical connection between you and him. I think it still continues to this day.

"Your daddy had a tender heart. He saw the good in everyone. He had many friends. He loved rainy days and cozy places. He loved wrapping up in quilts, wearing flannelette pajamas. He loved going to the show and taking baked potatoes to eat. He would buy little bags and sometimes big bags of candy at 7-11 when he didn't think I knew. He loved pistachio nuts and jujubes. When he was a young boy, he played Daddy Warbucks in his school play of *Annie*. He sang and danced and said his lines with such confidence. He presented Annie with a bouquet of red roses when the play was over. He had motorcycles and pickup trucks. He loved people and had fun at parties. He wore bright yellow shirts, orange ones too. He never forgot my birthday. He cried at sad movies and sad moments in life.

"He wanted to add to this world and he did. He was a man you could proudly call your dad."

Time marched on. Soon 2007 turned into 2008. It was a year that would bring tremendous challenges and three more of our family members would leave this world.

In 2008, my sister, Jo, was forced to walk my path. Her daughter, Michelle, got an infection, which travelled to her brain. She was transferred to Kamloops to be treated by a neurosurgeon. She arrived unconscious. She underwent brain surgery to drain the infection from her brain. She recovered well and was up and walking within a week. She was on IV antibiotics and scheduled to return home. The morning she was to be discharged, the hospital phoned and said she was found unconscious and needed to be put on a ventilator. When we arrived at the hospital, the neurosurgeon said her brain had herniated into the brain stem and there was no hope for her survival. When the brain herniates, it means either swelling or bleeding produces pressure inside the skull. This causes the brain to be displaced. It was such a shock because she'd been doing so well. Michelle, at the age of thirty-eight, was taken off life support the next day. The whole family was there as she took her last breath. My poor sister was inconsolable. Michelle left three teenage children.

It was hard to watch my sister live through the following days. They were all too familiar. I knew I couldn't help her. This may sound harsh, but I knew she had to find a way to survive, just as I had. The strongest lesson I've learned is that no one can do the work for you, as much as we want to take the pain away. She only had a month of grieving before our mother passed at the age of eighty-nine. Jo had been hit with two deaths within one month and she would soon endure yet another one only eight months later.

Tyler, Jo's middle child, contracted pneumonia. It happened in 2009, just when the H1N1 flu was at its worst. Tyler's immune system wasn't strong so he was unable to fight the virus. He died in April 2009 at the age of forty-one.

I cannot put into words the feelings I had after these three deaths. Two of my sister's children were gone in a short eleven months, with my mother in between. I wasn't sure Jo would survive. It was as if she was drowning in her sorrow. At times she would bob to the surface, only to be pulled under by the riptide of her grief. She had always been a strong woman, but I was terrified this was too much for her. Her life force was weak and I was afraid she was going to give up.

But I watched as she put one foot in front of the other. She survived and, to this day, continues to be a strong woman. I have such respect for her.

Jo and I began our families with five children. Now we have two between us, the oldest and the youngest. And life goes on.

Part Three:
This is Who I Am Now

CHAPTER 6

Death and Dying, Life and Living—a Course Is Born

As the next few years passed, I continued to teach. I worked to make the courses better each year. I believed I had an obligation to my students to make sure the information I taught was current and evidence based. The field of nursing changes very rapidly as new technology, science and research inform the practice. It's never static. The ever-changing nature of the profession fascinated me.

It was also fun to create new ways to deliver the course material. I researched teaching methods and found ways to bring the theory alive with experiential classroom activities. The creation of real-life situations provided a strong platform for the academic theory. It was during this time, I began thinking about how I could integrate more death and grief theory into the main nursing courses. Some was already there, but I knew I needed to do more work to inform myself on the various aspects of grief theory. Death was a reality for the students, both personally and professionally, but there is not a lot of time spent on studying the subject. I had only skimmed the surface in my education. So I decided to make this the focus of my master's work. The more I researched, the more I wanted to know.

The study of death, dying and bereavement is called "thanatology." It was interesting to me that I had lived all of these things but didn't fully understand what had happened to me. I began to identify many of my own responses in the literature. I could see how valuable this understanding was and wanted to share what I had learned. I could see the value of creating a full course on thanatology.

I had no experience writing a course, but the challenge tempted me. It seemed right, so I began the first steps in designing the material. My mind danced with possibilities. I had a hard time sleeping because I would wake up in the middle of the night with an idea and would have to write it down. I felt a familiar passion coursing through my veins. I thrived on learning and realized I had taken a sabbatical to work with my own grief. I would never have had the energy or interest if I hadn't respected the need to grieve. It had been the hardest work I'd ever done but the time had been so necessary to allow me to proceed with living. I didn't know it at the time, but I could see it now. I could easily have become lost if I hadn't honoured the need to grieve the loss of Jamie. In doing so, I was ready to step forward and work with others to understand how death can be a part of life. It's not that we "get over it"; we learn to weave it into our lives. I wouldn't have known this if I hadn't lived it.

In our society, we tend to avoid death until we have to face it. As nurses, steeped in this societal avoidance, we're expected to effectively deal with death, dying and grief in our work. But we are often not prepared to do this. As I pondered this thought, I knew I had to keep working to develop this course. It was going to be a great deal of work, but I was motivated by two experiences I'd had with patient death.

My first experience started my interest in death and dying. I was a nursing student and witnessed my first patient death. It hit me hard. I will call the patient Sarah (not her real name) to protect any possible identification.

Lying in the hospital bed, Sarah took her last breath as I sat with her and held her hand. I had never seen a dead person in my life and yet I watched as this woman left this world.

How can this be? I thought. *I was just talking to her and now she's gone.* I felt such strong emotions: anger, sorrow, awe, guilt for feeling awe, and disbelief. I knew intellectually that people die, but emotionally and spiritually, it was so powerful.

I sat with Sarah for a long time. She had no family, but she didn't die alone. She died with me. I was a stranger, and yet, we shared a very intimate moment—when life left her body. It was as if the light went out inside and she became a mannequin, like the ones you see in store windows. A couple of moments before she was breathing and her heart was beating. She was alive, just like me. Now she was dead, just like I would be one day.

I stood up and began the ritual nurses perform when a patient dies. I had memorized the steps from my textbook so it provided a sense of order for my chaotic mind. As I listened to her chest, my tears began to fall. They were for her and they were for me. Many years ago, Sarah had been someone's child. And now she was gone. I stood up and went to find my instructor.

My instructor was busy helping other students, so I waited until she was available. I briefly told her what had happened. She listened for a few moments and then told me death was a part of nursing and I needed to get used to it. She warned me I was getting too attached to my patients. I needed to maintain a professional distance and not get too involved. I knew she believed what she was saying, but I was devastated with her thoughts. I had been so certain she would understand how I was feeling. But she didn't. She had her own perspective and believed she was helping me. I couldn't stop thinking about it. I found myself wondering if I was too sensitive to be a good nurse. I knew I would be faced with death many times in the next few years. How was I going to handle it? Would I be sad every time a patient died? I was swimming in a sea of questions and didn't know who could help me. So I stuffed the feelings down and continued with my day.

The second experience was an incident with a nursing student, Pat (not her real name). I was her nursing instructor. Pat had been working with a patient who was at the end of her life. After my own experience as a student, I always made sure I included seminar time for students to discuss their ideas, fears and anxiety about working with patients who were dying. We also explored their feelings about grief and how they could effectively work with families who were experiencing loss. It certainly wasn't enough preparation, but I hoped it would help when students had to face the death of a patient.

As Pat's patient grew weaker and closer to passing away, we spent time talking about her feelings. She said she felt prepared to care for her patient as she died. Then one day, it happened. I was helping another student when Pat approached me to tell me her patient had died. I stepped out into the hallway and spent a few minutes talking with her. She assured me she was fine and asked if she could wrap and transport her patient to the morgue. She would have the help of two other experienced nurses. I knew them well because I had worked with them for years on the floor and they would be empathetic towards Pat's first brush with death. So I agreed she could work with them. The day ended with a student conference as it always did. Pat shared her experience of caring for a deceased patient and she appeared to have had handled it well.

The next week Pat was not in class. She did not show up for her shift at the hospital. She didn't respond to my emails or phone messages. None of the other students had seen or spoken to her. I was worried. Her emergency phone contact was her mother. When I called, she assured me Pat was fine but not able to come to school.

Three weeks later Pat showed up at my office unannounced. She started to cry as soon as she sat down. She said, "I'm dropping out of the nursing program. I can't do this work. I'm not meant to be a nurse."

After a few minutes, she began to tell me what had happened when preparing her patient for the morgue. She had been fine washing and wrapping the body in the plastic shroud. She helped transfer onto the morgue stretcher. Just as she and the other nurses began moving the stretcher out of the room, the patient's hand slipped out of the shroud and dangled off the edge of the stretcher. Pat had stared in disbelief. The wedding ring on her patient's hand was just like her grandmother's ring. She had been very close to her grandmother, who had recently died. The ring was an unforeseen trigger that sent Pat reeling into her unresolved grief over her grandmother's death. She said it immobilized her. She had literally stepped out of her life for the past three weeks. She had isolated in her apartment, unable to eat or sleep. She said all she did was cry.

We talked for a long time. In that moment, I knew I had to find a way to bring more death education into my own nursing practice as a faculty member. It wasn't enough to find teachable moments to address the impact of death. I knew I would need to do my own research before I attempted to help others. I wasn't sure how I was going to do this, but I knew I wanted to try. The nursing curriculum was already packed full and didn't have sufficient room to explore such a broad topic.

Death is everywhere in nurses' work. From death before a baby is born, right up to death of a senior and everything in between. And yet, the nursing textbooks dedicate very few pages to the subject of death and grief.

And so, the idea of an elective course began taking shape in my mind. I would call it *Death and Dying, Life and Living*. How could I make that happen? I knew I could handle the course content, but I was unclear if I could navigate the students' response. I saw it as a considerable responsibility. The subject matter, death and grief, carried a powerful charge. It could be very personal. I wondered if students would actually want to take a class on death and dying. I did a little research and discovered many students who do enrol in such a course often have had loss in their own personal lives. Some had experience with suicide, either thinking about it themselves or knowing someone who completed suicide. The more time I spent in the literature, the more I knew I had only just scratched the surface in my own education. My knowledge was limited to the most current theories. I couldn't wait to get started examining what had been written about thanatology. It was a fascinating walk and allowed me to burrow deeply into the literature. I loved every moment of the learning and over the next year or so that was all I wanted to do.

During that time, Jamie poked his voice into my thoughts many times. He reminded me I could assist others by creating a platform to explore issues many people struggle with. He told me that, if I was brave enough to step forward and promote the class, it might help others process their grief so they could help others in their own lives and in their work setting. It would be like a pebble in a pond creating larger and larger circles. He said my own grief, both personal and professional, would bring the theory to life.

I was so excited when I began my final paper in the master's program. In the paper, I presented two different avenues for the teaching. The first one was based on integration of death, dying and bereavement into the courses already offered by the School of Nursing. The second was a standalone elective course. I liked the second idea. I took a deep breath and approached the dean of the nursing program with the idea. She was very open and helped me prepare my idea for presentation to the university.

I needed to go before a group of my peers and explain why this course was important. This was not a comfortable thing for me to do. I found it quite intimidating, but I knew I had to present my case in a convincing and organized way. After asking numerous questions, they approved moving forward with the course. I was so happy. I literally floated out of the meeting. It was actually becoming a reality.

I had requested the course be interdisciplinary. My research revealed our Western society avoided talking about death. As a rule, we sequester it until we have to look at it when a friend, family member or pet dies. I knew that, even though I'd been present for many deaths in my nursing career, nothing had prepared me for Jamie's death. I was absolutely lost in my pain. I didn't know what was happening to me and had no idea how to navigate the first few weeks or months. And I didn't know where to turn.

I began to wonder if it would have been more bearable if I'd learned more about grief before it happened. I would have found comfort in knowing I wasn't losing my mind. When I started to write the course I had these thoughts in mind. They were also the beginning ideas for this book. If a person could compare their own experiences to the knowledge of those who had studied and written about this subject, would it help with their suffering? I was in a perfect position to see how this worked by conducting the work with students.

Nursing students have to face death and grief in their work. I could see where other programs such as respiratory therapy, social work and psychology could benefit from studying thanatology. The literature written in all these disciplines discussed the lack of education for these students. It was true of medical students and first responders too. I knew offering an interdisciplinary approach was the way to go.

I began working on the course content; it came together quite easily. There would be a theory piece and an experiential piece. The lessons began with learning about how we were all steeped in the same societal marinade that avoided death. It was important for the students to examine their own feelings of grief and loss. I wanted to stimulate group conversations, sharing ideas and questioning. So I built case studies of actual events into the lessons based on theoretical situations as well as real life ones from my own nursing practice. The discussions were rich. They would be complemented by personal stories when individuals chose to tell their own story.

Finally, I was ready for the first class. An idea had come to me one day about how to begin the course. It brought out a strong creative surge. I was excited but at the same time anxious because it was an unorthodox way to teach. I arranged for a colleague to take the first hour for me. She told the students I was unfortunately called away. This was not true. I was in the girls' bathroom getting ready to enter the classroom. I wore a long flowing black dress. I put a garland of black fabric flowers around my neck and placed a big black feather in my hair on a pin.

Complete with a black feather boa and a black rose in my hand, I walked down the hall to the classroom. I had dressed as death. You can imagine the looks I received. In my mind I was thinking, *Oh my God, I can't believe I'm doing this. This is taking a big risk.*

It was very overwhelming for me because I had always gone to great lengths to make sure I didn't draw attention to myself. But Jamie's death had changed that. I found myself more willing to take chances. I discovered I had a sense of humour and was looking forward to the debut of my acting career. I had never felt quite so alive. I was following my inner guidance, which told me I needed to do this.

I knocked on the classroom door.

My colleague answered. "What do you want?" she asked.

"I am death," I said. "I was told to come to this room."

"Death has no place in a university," she answered. "You might want to try visiting the hospital or hospice. They have death there."

I stepped further into the room. I will never forget the look on the faces of the forty people sitting in the desks. Most of them looked stunned. They later told me they didn't know what to think.

Then I said, "Has anyone been touched by death in this room?" Many raised their hands.

I walked to the front of the room. "Well," I said, "you didn't think this would be an ordinary class, did you?"

I still smile when I think about that first day in 2006. It was the beginning of the most rewarding work I have ever done.

Over the next ten years, I taught hundreds of students. It was everything I had hoped it would be. Those who registered brought their own wisdom and unique perspectives. The dialogue was rich; the feelings shared were powerful. The culture was one of curiosity, respect and intellectual stimulation. We all learned from one another and that was just what I had pictured happening.

After a few years, I was asked to add a summer offering along with the winter one. The diversity of the student population grew. There were nursing, tourism, psychology, respiratory, social work and journalism programs all represented. And sometimes others from the outside community took the course. Various cultural groups were drawn to the work, and their various perspectives on death, grief and rituals brought an authentic voice to the subjects. The students were the main ingredient that made the course successful. I had the privilege of guiding the process, but they were the threads that created the outstanding fabric of the experience. There were a variety of areas outlined in the syllabus for us to cover in each semester offering. Some of the learning activities involved going out into the community.

When we studied hospice and funerals, we went together to visit both facilities. It gave everyone a first-hand opportunity to see what it felt like to walk in the door. We would always follow up with discussion after each visit. Most had never been to either a hospice or a funeral home. Those who had were often able to share what it had been like for them when the visits involved people they loved. It was very different to enter when it was part of a class project. The emotional reaction of going when family or friends were dying was discussed. In this way, the ones in the class taught others valuable lessons from their past experiences.

I always tried to tie in the visits with the concepts we were studying. We would consider elements of a funeral and then, sometimes in groups, students would plan a funeral on paper. They were always amazed at how much work and details were involved and said it was like planning a wedding.

I suggested after such an exercise they go home and open the conversation with their families to investigate potential wishes about advance directives and funeral arrangements. Most often, the conversation had never happened in their family, and it was very interesting to hear when they came back to class the reactions they'd encountered. These conversations can be difficult, but in my experience as a nurse, I've seen families torn apart trying to decide what their loved ones might have wanted after they've died. Family members don't always come to consensus on such matters as cremation versus burial or no service versus a funeral, and it can create great anxiety at a time when everyone is grieving. After these things were explored, we would visit the funeral home. Sometimes the funeral director would take us on a tour of the casket room, the viewing room and the chapel. They would answer any questions students might have. Sometimes the visit included a walk through the room where bodies were prepared for embalming. The questions created by this activity flowed endlessly, and the directors always handled this with dignity and respect for the work they did.

I also asked everyone to visit a local cemetery. I had an outline of what to look for to help guide the process. It was interesting to hear the insight gleaned from such an exercise. There was much reflection and discussion the next time we met. A common theme from the discussion was the surprise at how peaceful the cemetery was. A comment I often heard was that they'd always associated a dark feeling with places where people were buried. But instead many said they had a feeling of calmness as they wandered through the grounds.

With all of these community activities, students were always given the option of not participating. I knew the visits might seem unorthodox—and they were—so I never wanted anyone to feel obligated just because it was part of the course activities. I called these visits "enrichment" so it didn't sound mandatory. The funny thing is, I never had a student miss a visit unless they were sick.

Every year I looked forward to the beginning of the semester. I began to realize there were common themes in those who enrolled. Most had a strong appetite to study and apply learned information to their own lives and professions. They seemed to enjoy the practical aspects, such as learning how to communicate with those experiencing death and grief, and how to write a eulogy and a sympathy message. They actively applied the grief theories to their own past experiences and made meaning of what had happened. The strong thirst for this knowledge made the teaching piece incredibly satisfying for me.

The course dedicated two full weeks to concentrate on grief. It's such a broad subject. Here is an outline of some of the main areas we looked at.

Grieving styles

Grief can affect men and women differently. I always jokingly used the statement "all Canadians love hockey" as an example of a common belief. "But," I'd say, "we know not all Canadians love hockey." So too the theory of men and women's grief is not an absolute but does tend to apply to many.

Grief can be personified as feminine or masculine, but variations can be wide. Researchers Kenneth Doka and Terry Martin[9] studied grieving styles—they describe intuitive and instrumental grievers. Intuitive grieving is centred around feeling and expressing emotion and can be seen as a feminine model. Instrumental grieving involves separating the mind from the emotions so there's a lack of external emotions; this explains how problem solving and practical issues dominate in this masculine model. These are grieving styles more than gender issues. I identified with the intuitive style as I spent the first few weeks of my mourning crying pretty well non-stop, and I found myself talking to others and sharing my deep emotions. Greg, on the other hand, focused on the legal matters. He was the one to obtain Jamie's death certificate and book the church for the Celebration of Life. He wanted to do. I wanted to be.

When these grieving styles were introduced in the classroom, many of the students gave their own examples of how they saw people in their lives react. For the most part, it seemed Doka and Martin were quite accurate. There is also another category—dissonant grieving style. Here the two styles are mixed. So there is a mix of what happens when a person grieves, a combination of intuitive and instrumental.

Four phases of grieving

Another important area of study involved phases in mourning. John Bowlby[10] writes about four phases of grieving:

Shock and numbness

---

[9] Kenneth J. Doka and Terry L. Martin, *Grieving beyond gender: understanding the ways men and women mourn* (New York: Routledge, 2010).

[10] Bowlby, *Attachment and loss.*

Yearning and searching

Disorganization

Reorganization

I found this theory very helpful.

Bowlby describes the first phase as being in a dazed state, stunned. I can remember on that first day after Jamie's death feeling very unreal. It was like I was looking through a thick fog. I couldn't focus. I felt numb. Even when the critical incident helper took me outside, she had to encourage me to move my feet. She said, "one foot in front of the other," like I was learning to walk. And, in so many ways, as I look back, I was learning to walk in a new world.

The second phase, yearning and searching, involves wanting things to be the same as before the person died. There's an unwillingness to accept what has happened. This happened to me when I kept thinking Jamie was going to walk up the driveway. I would find myself thinking I would phone him about something that had happened in my life. Other times I thought I saw him—in the grocery store, head bent, picking up a head of lettuce. I would almost call his name and then remember the reality. The back of a man's head in front of me in the bank lineup looked like Jamie's hairline and I almost tapped him on the shoulder. Then I would remember and catch myself. When I went out to the accident scene and combed through the things left behind on the grass, I was searching for something that would say it wasn't Jamie who had died there. These things were all pieces of yearning and searching.

In the classroom, students often raised their hands to offer stories of their own. I think it brings comfort to know it's not uncommon for these things to happen. It's rarely discussed because there seems to be elements of shame in telling others who haven't experienced this phenomenon.

The third phase is disorganization and despair. It's a time when you can no longer deny the person has passed. Self-identity is challenged. When I was asked by strangers about the number of children I had, I didn't know what to answer. Was I still Jamie's mother? Did I still have two children? Do I say, "I have a son, Sean, and had another child, Jamie, but he died." If I did this, others would immediately tell me how sorry they were that they'd asked and they would find a reason to keep moving on their way. I always felt so badly, but if I didn't acknowledge Jamie, I felt like I wasn't respecting the fact that he lived a life. You never think of these things until you're faced with them. It was difficult to keep moving forward when the unexpected popped up on a regular basis. Sometimes I questioned my own sanity. I've talked to many people over the years. The stories they tell me tend to have a similar flavour. That's why it's important to be able to talk to other people about these things. It makes you feel less alone.

The final phase is reorganization. In this phase, a "new normal" is hopefully found. Living in this world without the deceased person becomes the work. It's hard work, but on some level, you know it has to be done. I remember thinking, *Jamie wouldn't want me to get lost permanently in my sorrow. The best way to honour his life is to live mine.* My fear was that, in doing this, I would have to let him go. I know better now.

Four tasks of mourning

Another very helpful tool for understanding the grief process is psychologist J. William Worden's[11] tasks of mourning model. He provides a framework of four tasks worthy of consideration when a person is in mourning:

Accept the reality of the loss

Process the pain of the grief

Adjust to a world without the deceased

Find an enduring connection with the deceased while embarking on a new life

These elements help us understand how dealing with grief is a process not a destination.

To accept the reality of the loss isn't always a person's first reaction especially if the death was sudden. There's a period of time when it seems very unreal. In my own case, I remember thinking it couldn't be possible. *There has to be some mistake. Another car was involved in the accident. Maybe he*

---

[11] J. William Worden, *Grief counseling and grief therapy: a handbook for the mental health practitioner*, 4th ed. (New York: Springer Publishing, 2009).

wasn't actually driving the car. Someone else might have been behind the wheel.
The mind has a way of sheltering the initial shock. At times, it takes viewing
the body for the truth to set in.

The second task, process the pain of the grief, can be very hard to do. In
the beginning, the pain can feel overwhelming; the intensity can overshadow
any other thought. To escape the pain, some turn to alcohol or drugs—just
to get some relief. But unfortunately, grief just patiently waits.

In class, I would say, "While a person puts the pain on hold, grief works
out at the gym developing strong muscles. One way or another the pain of
grief will surface because it still lives inside the person."

Even years later, it doesn't go anywhere. It is still waiting for a chance to
be expressed. In the first few days of my grief, my doctor wanted to give me
sedatives, but I refused. At the time I hadn't studied grief in detail so I didn't
learn I had to feel the pain. I just knew there was no back door and the only
way was to feel it. And I did. There are no words for the depth of despair I
felt. But after some time had passed, the pain lessened. I didn't think it was
possible, but it was. It's unrealistic to think anguish can continue at the same
initial level. A person could not survive for long like that. This phase allows
the grief to be processed and integrated into the bereaved person.

When a person dies, those remaining family members and friends begin
to take on new roles. They learn to move ahead in life and the daily tasks of
living are addressed. The third task begins by learning to adjust to a world
without the deceased. It takes time and a great deal of energy. I know. I
had many days where I just wanted to hide from the world. But I knew I
couldn't do this forever so I began to step out into life again. Returning to
work helped me with this task.

Over the weeks following Jamie's death, we shut down the ward. I found
my memory and concentration were not always sharp. This is common in
grief. I put reminders on sticky notes so I could keep things straight. My desk
fluttered with tiny little yellow flags, but they created a compass to navigate
through my workday. It's not unusual for grieving people to find it hard to
concentrate. It's a normal part of the process.

My inner voice became my true north and slowly I could feel trust seeping
back into my life. With little baby steps, I set sail to discover my new normal.
I found when I was unsure of the next step, I would go back into the silence

of my mind. Each time I did, the answer was always waiting. It was like I tuned into heaven's radio station. When I blocked out the outer world, I found the rich inner landscape of my own truth.

For me, going back to work helped. It wouldn't be right for everyone, but I suppose, in a way, it was part of the instrumental style of grieving previously mentioned. Getting up in the morning and getting out of the house helped me gradually start reaching out for some sense of normalcy. It was good to have something to do. I also began seeing friends again. It wasn't easy to do because I have to admit I was envious they all had their children alive. It made me feel very alone, but as time went on, it got better.

The final task is to find an enduring connection with the deceased as you embark on a new life. Jamie helped me with this task. The words that came through during his interactions with me were so beneficial. I didn't have to erase his memory to feel normal again. I knew I had lost "normal" when he took his last breath. I had to find a new way to operate in the world, but at the same time, I wanted to find ways to keep his memory alive.

Continuing bonds of love

I did find a very helpful tool and realized I could still stay connected. This tool is called "continuing bonds" and was researched by Dennis Klass, Phyllis Silverman and Steven Nickman,[12] among others. There's a lot written about maintaining an ongoing relationship with the person who's died. They remain in the inner life of the person who's grieving. It creates a feeling of solace and comfort for many people. It did for me.

There are many ways to do this, and each person needs to find what's meaningful for them. Certainly the transmissions I received from Jamie are an example of continuing bonds. After-death communication has been reported by many people. I found this to be true in the classroom. Students spoke of a fragrance, sometimes flowers or smoke, or perhaps a favourite perfume scent, that would suddenly come into their awareness. They reported the fragrance would immediately make the deceased person feel closer. Other students spoke of numbers appearing in sequence, such as the telephone number

---

[12] Dennis Klass, Phyllis R. Silverman and Steven L. Nickman, eds., *Continuing bonds: new understandings of grief* (Washington, DC: Taylor and Francis, 1996).

111-111-1111 that came up on our home phone during Jamie's Celebration of Life or the clock showing 1:11 or 11:11. That came up many times in my conversations with others. Other things I found that created a bond included planting an apple tree with friends and baking a pie each Thanksgiving from the apples. On holidays, I light a single white candle and include Jamie in the celebrations that way.

I've heard others talk about creative ways to keep memories alive. One way is to use a loved one's recipes; each time they're used, a connection is made. Others continue the life work of the person who's died. Or they donate to the person's favourite charity. So many ways to remember someone who was special in your life. My husband plants dusty millers and alyssum each year in memory of his father. They seem like simple gestures, but they're effective in maintaining a relationship with those you love.

At one time in history, it was felt you had to somehow forget the person who died so you could stop grieving. We know now grieving is something to integrate into the tapestry of your life. Your relationship with someone doesn't just end when they die. It carries on in memory and perhaps in continuing bonds. Death may end a life, but it doesn't have to end the relationship. A father is always a father. A son is always a son. There is comfort in that thought.

CHAPTER 7

Lessons Learned

And so here we are. Over eighteen years since the accident and I am ready to finish this story. I talk to Taylor on a regular basis. She has turned into such a lovely young person, almost nineteen years old. She carries much of the wisdom her father did. She cares about the world and what happens, like Jamie did. She's a caring, loving and compassionate person. She has grown up knowing about Jamie and the life he lived. It's part of her heritage. I have always seen her for who she is rather than as a replica of Jamie. Somehow I think that would be an unfair burden for her.

Since 2002, I've met many parents who have lost children. There's a strange kind of comfort when you discover someone else who has walked the road you've walked. There's a knowing in their eyes. We have different stories because we had different relationships, different children, but that look conveys what a thousand words could never express. It's a silent salute to the battle they know you have fought and continue to fight.

As I look back ...

Time has passed. As I look back, I can see there were lessons I learned through that time. Here they are, in no particular order:

Grief is necessary

Everyone is different

Don't let society tell you how to respond

Find ways to self-soothe

It gets better

Making meaning is an important part of grief

Grief can bring a new-found freedom

Belonging is a natural need

Taking care of yourself takes work and dedication to self

Let's look at them in more detail.

Grief is necessary

Grief is hard work. It occupies every corner of your life, especially in the beginning. It's relentless and chases you no matter how fast you run. You may think you can outsmart it, but in the end, it finds you. It may be delayed, but grief will keep knocking on your door until you answer.

The work is not to get over it or around it. The work is to find a way to weave the loss into your life tapestry. It becomes part of who you are. It changes you in so many ways. You're not the person you were before the loss happened. How could you be? Your identity has been altered. Take an active part in your grief instead of passively observing from a distance. Honour your pain. Tell your story over and over again until it loses some of its sharp edges. I know our culture shies away from the grief of others, but … you have a right be heard.

I learned how strong I was through the process of grief. I wouldn't have known this unless I'd been so violently challenged. I survived my greatest nightmare. But in surviving, I had to give myself the gift of my grief before I could continue living my life.

Even to this day, grief still plays a quiet melody in the background. It's not loud and demanding as it was, but I still know it's there. It got the attention it deserved and now it's content to blend into my history. I had to find a place for it in my life or I believe it had the power to destroy me. We have a silent truce now, a subtle understanding. Grief was the ransom I had to pay for loving Jamie. It's the necessary price you pay. It was well worth the pain to have had Jamie a part of my life.

Everyone is different

Grief is universal. It's painful in all cultures and genders and has a common language for all of us. Yet, while it's universal, the relationships are unique to each person.

Most people voice anxiety when trying to comfort a person in mourning. Sometimes we avoid the situation at all cost, afraid we might say the wrong thing. But the grieving person is isolated at a time when they need community the most. Yes, it's awkward to know what to say. I've heard others say things like "I know how you feel" or "I lost my mother too. I know your loss." Even with the best intentions, this tends to diminish the story the other person is trying to tell.

No one knows the experience for another person. To me, it's disrespectful to assume I know. Each relationship is individual, even within families. Two brothers may view the loss of their father in very different ways. It's because their perceptions are their own.

If a mother tells me about losing her child, I don't begin to think I know her situation. I have empathy for her, but my own story needs to stay out of the conversation. In the moment, it's her story that needs to be told. There are times where self-disclosure may be beneficial but not when the other person needs to speak. Storytelling is an important part of making meaning. I have learned to talk less and listen more.

Sometimes a person may just need your presence. A few years ago, as a hospice volunteer, I was asked to visit the hospital to see a person who was dying. When I got there the patient asked to meet me in a private meeting room.

"How can I help?" I asked.

"Please sit down," she said. "I need you to stay with me as I cry. I can't cry in front of my family because it upsets them too much."

For the next hour, I sat across from her and she quietly cried. There was no conversation. She dried her eyes, thanked me for coming and then left the room. I never saw her again. My job had been to bear witness to her suffering. I felt very privileged to have been trusted to do this.

It's also important to not assume you know what a grieving person needs. Sometimes they themselves may not even know. You may be surprised to find out the person wants to be left alone. That was true for me. It was good to know others were available if I changed my mind, but I knew it was in the silence I could connect with my soul and find comfort in my own inner voice. It told me what to do and how to navigate the first days and weeks. I was guided to have a hot stone massage during the first week. The idea came to me one night and I found a spiritual practitioner. The ritual of placing the stones on my forehead and down my body was so perfect for me. It filled a primal need I didn't even know I had. The silence allowed me to hear the guidance from beyond my grief. It helped keep me sane.

When you are the one grieving, follow what feels right for you. Remember you have never walked this path. You may have lost someone before, but this is the first time for you to lose this particular person. Each experience feels different. Communicate to others what you need and don't be afraid to ask for help.

If you are supporting another person who has had loss in their life, allow them to guide what they need. It might be as simple as just sitting with them. It could involve you buying groceries or running errands if the person can't find the energy to do it themselves. You might be asked to contact family and friends to pass on the information about the death and any planned gathering. Perhaps check back with the person after a few days. Even watering the garden or spending time with their children might be just what is needed.

Don't let society tell you how to respond

There are expectations in society about how people should grieve and how long it should last. Every situation is different. When I went back to work after three weeks, it seemed odd to some people. They thought I should stay home, but I needed to go. It was right for me and I knew it. Others may delay return to work for many months. Some may never go back to their previous occupations. None of this is right or wrong. It depends on each person's own truth for what is right for them.

People may find pictures of the deceased person comforting and decide to keep many photos out around the house. Pictures may be too painful to look at every day and are placed in a drawer. Perhaps they will be brought out again at a later date. Again, it depends on the individual. Some of us keep clothes and personal items and others need to get rid of everything associated with the other person.

Time has no linear meaning in grief. Sometimes you will see tears of sorrow many years, many decades after a death. The tears can be triggered by an event or a memory. At times, we may not know what prompted the tears. We don't "get over" the loss of a loved one. We learn to live with the loss the best we can. There will be times when emotions run high no matter how long it's been. Don't let others tell you how your grief should be.

Find ways to self-soothe

Think about what brings you comfort and make a list of these things. Grief is some of the hardest work we'll ever do. A warm bath, a long run, a good book, time spent with family and friends can ease some of the fatigue and heaviness. It might be music, time in nature or an afternoon nap.

Meditation is an essential tool for me and I spend time quietly examining my inner world. It wasn't easy at first. It was hard to be still; my mind resisted contemplation. It wanted to keep racing ahead instead of resting in the moment. But I kept at it and, after time, discovered a wonderful place that vibrated with healing energy and peace. It was hard to leave once I slowed down and entered this meditative state. It felt familiar, like coming home. In this place, I had no gender, no age, no history. It was a place of reconnection to my soul. I learned how to soothe myself. The world is still a challenging place, but I find comfort in my inner world of meditation and writing.

Meditation involves quieting the mind. Many years ago I took a course on mindfulness. I had no idea how to do this. I remember the instructor telling us there was no magic formula. All you have to do is close your eyes and be aware of your breath as it enters and leaves the body. She said many thoughts will try to enter at the same time but to just come back to the breath. It was very hard to do in the beginning. I had a hard time sitting still for more than five minutes. I would sit on my hands until the timer went off. But slowly it got easier and I found I could continue for longer periods of time. When thoughts entered my mind, I would just acknowledge them and go back to concentrating on my breath. After a while, a sense of almost floating came over me and I drifted. If meditation is something you would like to try, with a little practice, you may find it very helpful during the acute grieving period. It could become a tool you can use for the rest of your life. There are many resources available if you would like to try this form of relaxation.

It gets better

The intensity of acute grief naturally lessens as time goes on. There's certainly no set schedule. It's different for everyone. In the beginning, I didn't know this. I thought I would feel the same from the day he died to my dying day. It's living each day that dulls the intensity of the first feelings. I find I'm careful to not visit the dark places. If I think back to the day in too much detail, I relive the pain. I have a choice about whether I do this or not. So I don't. I tenderly guide myself back to the present moment. I show myself compassion. There's nothing but sadness harboured in May 18, 2002.

Sometimes when the day is approaching, I feel a whisper of anxiety. I'm always glad when the day is over. Some years are good, but others can be unpredictable. Even years later, one or more of us may be feeling Jamie's loss more acutely. I always think of Taylor and text her to let her know she's on my mind. It must be so hard for her. She only knew Jamie for three months before he left. She has the stories of her father from all of us. I hope they help her.

Making meaning is an important part of grief

I found the hardest part of loss and grief is making meaning of what happened. There's a part of us that wants understanding. But in the beginning, it's beyond all understanding. Researcher Robert Neimeyer[13] suggests a central part of grieving is reconstructing meaning in your life after a significant loss.

---

[13] Robert A. Neimeyer, *Meaning reconstruction and the experience of loss* (Washington, DC: American Psychological Association, 2001).

Through my journalling, I slowly pieced together the mended version of my life. The connecting threads came to me once I had surrendered to Jamie's death. I no longer searched and yearned to find him. I accepted what had happened but found myself trying to design a life without him in physical form.

It was about this time that I had an unusual experience. Something larger than myself figuratively took me by the front of my shirt and spoke to me.

"Okay," it said, *"time to move on. Remember he was mine to begin with. I only lent him to you. I didn't have to give him to you at all. You enjoyed him for twenty-nine years. Be grateful for this. It could have been much worse. I could have had Sean in the car too. Or I could have allowed Jamie to live. You would have watched him suffer as the result of the fire. His beautiful body could have lived with disfigurement. He could have spent the next fifty years in a care home, in adult diapers, being fed, not able to move independently. But I didn't do this. I spared you the agony of watching this. So be grateful. Get on with your life."*

That powerful conversation with the Divine was a turning point for me. The nightmare of watching Jamie suffer for decades was worse than what I was experiencing in the moment. It somehow gave meaning to his death.

As a mother, the hardest thing is to watch your child in pain. If Jamie had lived with disfigurement and dependency, it would have destroyed me. In sharp contrast, I remembered the feeling of pure joy that he communicated to me shortly after his death. I had the sense he was euphoric wherever he was. What more could a mother ask for?

Grief takes time. It's a process. It's like being in a boat in the middle of the sea. Most of us aren't aware of the power of the ocean until we find ourselves in a very small boat in the middle of a storm. Grief is like that. We know death is real, just as the ocean is real. But it's such a shock when death knocks on our door and enters our life uninvited. We may have experienced small, maybe even moderate waves of challenge in our lives. We may think we're prepared for the impact of death. But I believe nothing prepares us for the magnitude of the waves death produces. The little boat called "My Life" was tossed around like a cork in an unforgiving ocean.

In the first few days and weeks, many people tried to rescue me from the aftermath of Jamie's death. I knew their intentions were good. The lifelines of food, flowers and cards reinforced I was not alone. I felt supported by the kind words and gestures. Most people struggle with the grief of others. They want to connect but carry the fear they'll say or do the wrong thing. The immensity of the death of a child hits others at a very primal level. If it could happen to Jamie, it could happen to their child. If it happened to me, it could happen to them. So as I tossed around in the never-ending waves produced by Jamie's death, I was aware of my family in their own private boats trying to stay afloat.

Our family tried to ride out the overwhelming pain by tethering our boats together so we wouldn't lose the connection. Although everyone had a different relationship—mother, father, brother, etc.—we all loved Jamie and struggled to be a family without the physical presence of one member. It reminds me of a baby's mobile that hangs over a crib. When all the parts of the mobile are placed perfectly, there's balance. But when one piece is removed, the mobile becomes lopsided. That's how it felt for our family—a piece was missing.

So we would plan dinners together and would tell the "Jamie stories." We laughed and we cried. As Sean talked, I discovered parts of Jamie's life I never knew about. Some parts of it I wanted to hear but some probably would have been better kept between brothers! But I could feel how healing it was for each of us to witness the experiences of the other family members. There was validation of each unique relationship.

Then one day, you wake up and the waves don't seem so daunting. The worst of the storm feels like it might have passed. You gingerly look around and see the bruised and battered lives of your family. You've all survived the initial days and weeks, maybe months or years. It's so different for each of us. There is no time frame, no recipe for grief.

But slowly it feels like you'll be able to pick up the oars and start reconnecting to life again. Piece by piece you make the repairs to your boat. The supplies needed for these repairs might be grief counselling, meditation or prayer. You might find exercise helps, along with time spent in nature. It also may help to set time aside to cry when you need to.

Then one day, you sense a crack of sunlight in the distance. *Could that actually be the sun?* It's been so long since you've seen it, felt the comforting warmth of its rays. You lift your face and feel the possibility of hope—hope that creates the foundation for a "new normal" and makes the present moment more bearable.

The path from the death of someone you love to the moment you feel a glimmer of hope is different for everyone. That's why we often feel so alone. Although the journey is uniquely ours, the pain we feel is universal. We all share a common denominator and a common goal.

The work of grief involves weaving the relationship with the deceased person into our lives. How you do that, only you know.

I was drawn to the lake. I would sit on the beach, behind my sunglasses and I would submit to the tears. They needed to be recognized. The rhythm of the waves lulled me somehow. Nature has a beautiful healing quality for everyone. There is wisdom in the natural kingdom of the outdoors.

Grief can bring a new-found freedom

I am a different person than I was. I have dropped the old dysfunctional clothes that harnessed me to pleasing everyone. When you are stripped down to the bare essentials in life, you also have an opportunity to redress yourself once you're ready. There is freedom in that.

I always thought I had to put others' needs before my own; that was essential to being a good person. After Jamie's death, I couldn't put others first. To survive, I had to concentrate on what I needed. First, I had to figure out exactly what that was as, throughout my previous life, I was in the habit of putting myself last. Well, not anymore! It's a work in progress, but at least the needs of others is no longer my default setting.

I remember saying to others, "I have nothing to give."

I think of life as a bank account. If you make enough deposits, you can make some withdrawals. The death of someone you love can totally deplete any reserve funds, no matter how large the bank balance may be. Grief is the biggest withdrawal most people make in a lifetime. The trick is to figure out how to maintain routine deposits after the loss. Much like a bankruptcy, you have to watch your money carefully—be careful where funds go.

After a death, it's important to look after yourself so you are capable of storing up some reserve. If you try lending some of yourself to fill the needs of others, you may find yourself with NSF messages coursing through your best intentions. So the people in your life may be left to find their own answers. In the end, that works better anyway. After a death, life is no longer what it was. We are forced to make changes.

There is freedom in redesigning your life, just like your wardrobe. You can throw out what doesn't fit anymore. If you've worn pastels in the past, you may find yourself ready for brighter colours. I know I was ready. Either I could continue with my black clothing of pain or I could shift to bright blues and greens. We all wear black in the beginning and we wear it for different lengths of time. There's no season limitation for black; it's never out of style for grieving.

One day you may wake up and tentatively add a coloured bracelet to wear with the black. You might question whether it's an appropriate fashion statement. If you listen very closely to that inner voice, you'll find the truth there. It doesn't matter what other people think. You have no one to please, no approval to seek.

The bracelet may be the first sign that tells you, "You will survive." It represents a glimmer of hope where none had existed before. It's the first ray of light in a world of shadow. Or you may decide you want to wear only black for a little longer. Society may tell you, "Enough time has passed." But you know you have not finished with black outfits yet. Some people never want to take off the black. They refuse to try a colourful bracelet or set of cufflinks. These folks may need a wardrobe consultant in the form of a grief counsellor to support them in selecting new accessories to wear in life.

As time goes on, you may find yourself adding more colour to your life. The black dress or suit always hangs in the back of the closet. There are times when you run your hands over the familiar fabric. It reminds you of your loss and your sorrow. You know that black outfit will never end up at the Sally Ann. You wore it through dark times. It's like a coat of armour but too heavy for you now.

There is freedom in choosing a new set of clothes, a new life. Standing naked in the world, stripped of innocence and security, you have earned the right to be anyone you want to be. I was once very quiet and, oddly enough, wore mostly black and brown clothes. I stayed in the background, didn't want to be seen. I had little confidence and tended to be somewhat anxious about life.

Now I wear bright colours every day. I am still humble, but I acknowledge my strengths. I fill my own needs, make deposits before withdrawals. And it started one day when I chose to add a colourful bracelet to my black dress of sorrow.

It amazes me that when death occurs, a universal experience, we often feel isolated from others. When we graduate, get married, have babies or retire, the landmark events are shared with others. Dying is really much the same as entering the world. We all do it. As a wise friend once said to me, "Each generation has a hundred percent mortality rate. No one gets away." And yet, often when a person is dying or when they're grieving, many find themselves alone. Why is that? Do we want to avoid the suffering of others? Do we think if we come too close, it might happen to us? Of course it will happen to us! And it will happen to those we love. Doesn't it make sense that we support each other? I think it does.

Belonging is a natural need

Each of us had company when we entered this world. A mother is required to be present for each birth. But when we die, there's no guarantee someone will be with us. Whether a life is long or very short, most people are connected, one way or another, to other people. It gives us a sense of belonging. It may be a family unit, but it could also be a group of people with no family ties. The connection to others provides the thread that tells us we are not alone.

Once a person has a loss, the social connections change. In a marriage or partnership, the loss suddenly renders you single instead of part of a couple. There's a feeling of not fitting in where you once stood in society.

The same is true of parents who experience the loss of a child. Intact families are a constant reminder of what you have lost. It's a different place to be. You don't belong any longer in what is considered a "normal family." You are the parent everyone is so fearful of becoming. Your sense of belonging vanishes. You are the odd man out, especially when you're at the beginning of your walk with grief.

It can be helpful to join a grief group, people who are experiencing something similar. In many cities, these groups are located in hospices and churches. It can be comforting to hear the stories of others and may provide some sense of belonging.

Even having informal discussions with others may be beneficial. In a world where grief stories are somewhat shunned, it can be comforting to be with others who understand what you're going through.

The death of a person most often affects the security of belonging. Grief is a healthy response to loss. It helps to share in a common way and is easier if you don't have to go it alone.

There are also unhealthy reactions to losing someone. Sometimes it can be a very solitary and lonely path. William Wooden[14] researched complicated grief and identified four categories:

Chronic grief reaction—grief lasts for an excessive length of time and the person may never come to terms with it. They have difficulty returning to life.

Delayed grief reaction—grief is not acknowledged or expressed at the time of the loss, but surfaces later, stimulated by an unseen trigger or subsequent death.

Exaggerated grief reaction—grief takes on an excessive quality and unhealthy coping may occur. Irrational fear or phobias can develop.

Masked grief reaction—a person can be seen as not grieving at all or exhibiting behaviour that doesn't seem part of the grieving response.

Generally these responses are due to the difficult nature of the relationship with the deceased or the circumstances surrounding how the person died. There may have been many deaths over a short period of time or perhaps the mourner has an underlying depressive condition that worsens after the death.

Taking care of yourself takes work and dedication to self

In the first few days and weeks following the death of someone you love, the work involved in acute grief can be very overwhelming. You may feel an obligation to other people. I can remember thinking I needed to keep a list of who gave me gifts following Jamie's death. Friends often left small things outside the front door or in the mailbox. Candles, music, books and flowers would appear. Cards and letters were also left, along with many, many items of food. I started a list with the full intention of writing thank you notes. But

---

[14] Worden, *Grief counseling.*

as the list grew, I realized I was not capable of keeping track. I was struggling with just living those first few weeks. I let it go without feeling guilty. It was the right thing for me to do.

For most of us, each death is unique because the relationship, the attachment, is different. You may have a very strong grief response when your dog dies. When your grandfather dies, you may find your response is less intense. It always comes back to attachment, how strongly you were connected to the deceased. The attachment is deep when you lose someone you strongly loved. Some people may not understand your response. As long as you do, that's what's important. If the acute stage of grief lasts longer than others think it should, stand by what it feels like to you. No one completely understands your experience as well as you do. Be guided by how you feel. This might be a new experience for many people. We're sometimes told how we should feel and take that for our own truth. If you can take the time to quiet the world down, you may find your own inner wisdom will bubble up in your consciousness.

The first summer following Jamie's death, I spent many hours at the lake. I found great comfort when I stood in the water up to my chin. It was soothing to both my body and mind. I knew I should go into the lake because I had become still inside and was guided to do this.

I also went into the forest. I hugged trees and felt their pulse vibrate in my own body. It brought me a small sense of security. The feel of the tree and its sheer size provided a soothing, solid reminder of the cycle of nature. I thought about how the roots penetrated deep into the earth and branches reached towards the sky. The trees stood strong in the wind and witnessed life and death on the forest floor. They grounded me. I gave thanks each time I hugged them. Steve Taylor[15] writes about transformation following bereavement. In his 2020 study, he identified characteristics found in many bereaved individuals:

A stronger appreciation for nature. Grieving seemed to increase awareness of the beauty and gift of the natural world. This was definitely true for me.

A decreased fear of death. Once they had lived through the death of their loved one, they found death didn't hold the power it once had. So many of us

[15] Steve Taylor, "Transformation through Loss and Grief: A study of personal transformation following bereavement," *The Humanistic Psychologist* (March 2020).

have death anxiety. It's understandable when you see how society avoids and denies death until it's on their front doorstep. When it actually arrives, there's a coming to terms with something most see as the enemy.

New values and perspectives arising out of the grief process. There was more value placed on more authentic relationships. For some, creating an open dialogue became easier. Patience also increased.

Altruistic endeavours overshadowed materialistic goals. Making the world a better place became important. The drive to accumulate material possessions dimmed in favour of working to help others.

Enjoyment of solitude. This was identified as a positive.

Nature and solitude were two things that helped me. They might help you too. If you tap into your inner resources and become still enough to listen, you may find your own unique answers. The main thing is to take care of yourself. This is often missed during bereavement. It's important to eat nutritional food even if you don't feel like eating. If possible, exercise. Even a short walk to the corner and back may make a difference to how you feel. It takes effort, especially when all you may want to do is go back to bed.

I try very hard to avoid the places in my mind that hold the most painful memories. These places include the days leading up to Jamie's death, the day he died, and the intense emotional time immediately following May 18, 2002. I still have the recording of his Celebration of Life, but I don't play it. All the many cards and letters are kept in a large Tupperware container under the stairs. Sometimes I will read a few. They remind me of the incredible support we received in those early months.

Family systems change when a member dies. The death of a spouse may create financial upheaval and role changes. The death of a child puts new pressures on the remaining family. Where there were two siblings, now there is one child. They may experience secondary losses throughout their life. They will be without a sibling to share the responsibility of older parents. They may not have other family members to share memories of the past with. They become an only child. You may fear upsetting people with an explanation that you have one child who died and another who is living. If you don't mention the deceased child, it may feel disrespectful to the life of that child. The same may be true for widows and widowers when they're asked, "Are you married?" When a spouse has died, it may not be clear, especially at first.

As time goes by, the pain begins to lessen. At first, I felt guilty I was living my life in spite of the loss. I can't remember the sound of his voice anymore. But I can still see his hands, the back of his neck, his crooked smile. Photographs help keep these images clear. But the sound of him, the touch of him and the scent of him—it's lost. Eighteen years later, the sound of him is like a distant echo. I know this is how it has to be. It's all part of the process of letting go of the earthly connection. I can't help but think that may be a good thing. If I was constantly reminded through all my senses, it would be very difficult to walk in this world.

There have been times over the years when I thought I felt him brush my cheek. It felt like a feather brushing gently against my face. Feathers appear in front of me on a regular basis. The feathers of a bird allow it to fly. So the feathers I find remind me Jamie is in flight. These thoughts are comforting. It would be so easy to give up and just endure life. No one would blame me. But if I allow earthly events, such as finding a feather, to enhance my everyday life, it becomes a gentler road.

It feels good to understand I am the designer of my reality. I can create the details as I want them to be. I can connect to him in spiritual form. I can no longer do this in a concrete sense as his body ceases to exist. As his mother, I need to connect on some level because otherwise he is truly gone. I couldn't live with that. The early connections brought an amazing amount of comfort. I understand now the reason I experienced spiritual rehearsals earlier in my life.

As I look back on my life, I can see where the pieces fit together. I can see how my life prepared me for what was to come. It's like a giant jigsaw puzzle. In the beginning, the pieces lie randomly on the table of possibilities. Soon some things begin to fall into place. As a young child I discovered that caring for my mother brought me great satisfaction. She wasn't a happy person, but I found ways to bring a smile to her face by picking up some of her daily chores. For a little while, I could pretend I had a normal family. This was especially true when all five of us sat down to eat something I'd prepared. Food brought us together in a way that nothing else seemed to. Caring for others became one of the jigsaw pieces.

I also found if I spent time in nature, I had an immediate positive reaction. The rope swing in the forest was my go-to place when storms were brewing at home. The trees cradled my soul as I swung back and forth in the energy of nature. The trees created a secret hiding place where no explanation was required; they just knew what I needed. I was safe.

Spending time in nature became a key puzzle piece in my evolving life. As a teenager, I found myself being drawn into the dense forest when I needed to put things in my life in order. Even when the pine trees in my backyard asked me if I would stay if Jamie left, I respected their wisdom. I had to argue with them for a while because I didn't like their message. I wanted to believe the message wasn't real, that I was just making it up. But they were relentless in their persistence. The trees were so deeply rooted in the earth, so grounded, I knew I had to give them an answer. Like an effective and caring parent, they insisted I was accountable. Those same trees sheltered and held me when I was crazy with grief. I hugged them like a child hugs a father or a mother. The pulse within them reminded me I was going to be okay, that I would survive life.

I also found cooking and caring for others penetrated the years as a wife and mother. Caring for my husband and sons became my salvation when challenges arose. In any marriage, there are times of turmoil, hurt feelings and misunderstandings. The smell of a carrot cake baking in the oven or the scent of freshly baked bread never failed to lift my spirits. It was a learned puzzle piece.

To this day, cooking is still one of the most enjoyable things I do. More importantly, it has the power to quell negative emotions. When I don't know what else to do, I cook! The recipe, the preparation of the ingredients, the aroma, the anticipation of tasting, all bring order in times of chaos. Even after Sean and Jamie moved out of the house, I continued to have a passion for creating gastronomic offerings for Greg. He remains to this day, my best recipe guinea pig. He loves most everything and is willing to try the most obscure combinations. Preparing food has seen me through some very stormy days.

I also volunteer at our local hospice as a cook. Once a week I spend a morning baking and making meals. It's very satisfying. Again I thank you, Mum, for being who you were and creating this legacy that I draw on even to this day! Since my time at hospice, I've talked to other volunteers and many say they're there because someone they loved died at hospice and they wanted to give back the care their loved one received. Others say it helps to work with patients and families when they're struggling with dying. I've heard them say they volunteer in honour of someone close to them who died.

As I look back, I can also see how school fit perfectly into my life. Going to school for the first time gave me an avenue of stability to follow. It provided a safe haven when things were unsettled at home. I rediscovered my love of learning when I went back to school to become a registered nurse. By submerging myself in learning, it helped when my sons left home to begin an independent life. As I began my life as an instructor at the college, I needed a master's degree. This work helped me through the overwhelming work of grief. It became a passion, a place to put my energy. I found myself working with students, and together we examined the sequestered subjects of death, dying and bereavement.

The jigsaw puzzle started to come together in a way I've only begun to see. The elements of nature, cooking, caring for others and school were cornerstones in my life—tools that I used throughout my life.

But there is still one more to discuss. Spirit. Without my spiritual life, I would not have been able to make sense of anything that happened. I have always been aware there's a mystery to life involving something bigger than me. I was introduced early to an "unseen something" just outside my reach. A scent wafting in the breeze like a forgotten memory. I have had many opportunities to experiment with remembering the mystery.

There is hope

The intent of this book is to offer hope. The world can seem very rocky, especially in these times we're living in right now. It can be hard to find something to hold on to, something to ground us. Our lives are full of challenges. The death of someone you love is one of the hardest.

When I first began writing, I had no idea I would end it by talking about COVID-19, the virus causing the global pandemic of 2020. I think it's safe to say no one saw this coming. We ended 2019 with a false sense of security that we knew the world we lived in. It's been said the pandemic is much like a death. The grief follows as we realize nothing will ever be the same. Just as a death in a person's life changes their world forever, global mourning can be seen each time we turn on the news or have conversations with others about the "new normal."

The same principles offered in the grief theories presented in this book can be applied to the world situation we find ourselves in today. The gradual adjustment to the truth behind physical distancing and mask wearing interferes with how life going forward will look. I stood outside our local grocery store last week and watched as people went in and out of the store. They lined up outside, standing on their designated circle to ensure two metres existed between them. There was a man in a security uniform counting people as they entered and left. Most people had a mask covering their face. If I didn't know better, I would think I was watching a science fiction movie. After the shock and numbness created at the beginning of the pandemic, society began to find a way to come out of their houses. But it's not the same; it's very different and will continue this way for a long time to come.

We yearn and search for a reality other than what we're looking at day to day. The cancellation of graduations, weddings, funerals, care home visitations, dances, wedding showers, church services and—especially hard—hugs with our families and friends. These rituals are at the very foundation of living and have been in place for hundreds of years. Some of us are not willing to play by the rules set out by health authorities. Perhaps that's part of the disorganization and despair outlined in the work of Bowlby. Society is shocked by the expectations and alterations required to keep the virus under control.

Hopefully reorganization will follow. This will require us to find a way to live with our new reality. We need to learn we cannot hold on to what was in our lives. It's hard work. Just as grieving is hard work. There are ways we can help ourselves. The tools used in the grief process can be used to balance feelings of fear and frustration. You can begin by decreasing the amount of news you watch in a day. It's important to be informed but not overwhelmed. Spending time in nature may be soothing, especially if it's combined with walking or running. There are many books and programs available to learn more about yoga, meditation and other spiritual practices.

Sharing feelings with friends and family may help to dilute anxious feelings. It's important to keep in touch, even if face-to-face visits still require physical distancing.

This is a time to reflect on values and beliefs. What is really important to you? The old world was based on conflict and competition. What do we want our new experience on earth to look like? Already we have evidence of compassion for humanity, and hopefully that will continue. At the present time, we're also hesitant to believe everything we hear. There are so many unknowns. As with each personal death we encounter in our own lives, we have to face the unknown and find avenues to weave new ways of living.

Some last words ...

The truth remains. Death is an ugly word. Even though I have found a way to live and enjoy my life, there's seldom a day that Jamie doesn't come into my thoughts. I would never want that to leave me.

Sometimes I smile when I see yet another white Honda Civic drive by on a neighbourhood street. I always say, "Hello, Jamie." Or I see 11:11 on the clock and decide he's taunting me from beyond the beyond. That's the fun part.

Then there are the moments that squeeze my heart and cause my eyes to brim with primal tears. They will always be there because he's still my son and I will always miss him. That's the ransom we pay for loving someone, and it's worth it.

CPSIA information can be obtained
at www.ICGtesting.com
Printed in the USA
BVHW032206140221
600125BV00001B/25